WHAT'S ON MY MIND?

A COLLECTION OF BLOG ENTRIES FROM
"OVERCOMING SCHIZOPHRENIA"

*****

WHAT'S ON MY MIND?

VOLUME 1

*****

ASHLEY SMITH

FOREWORD BY CHRISTINA BRUNI

What bloggers and other readers said about

Ashley Smith's blog

Overcoming Schizophrenia

I Choose to Live Award

Passionate Blogger Award

101 Blog Award

Disease.Com Top Blog Award

*****

"Well-written. Open and honest about living with this illness and helping others to cope and overcome daily issues. Informative for lay people to remove stereotypical beliefs and myths surrounding schizophrenia." Margaret

"Nice blog site. You provide a good look into a world that seems so closed off. Thank you." Rob

"Ashley, I just recommended your blog to another psychiatric hospital! Now, I know you are just a normal person with an incredible recovery to share and continue sharing. But I don't think you will ever know how many people you have encouraged!! You've definitely encouraged me." Anonymous

"This is instructive and informative blog on schizophrenia. As someone who also suffers from a psychotic illness I found it helpful to realize that I'm not alone and others have similar experiences..." Rachel

"Hi Ashley— your blog has been really helpful to me. I'm dealing with my wife's mental illness and reluctance to take meds— reading your writing gives me some perspective, something we all can use. Thanks." Anonymous

"I read this post two times. I like it so much, please try to keep posting." Henry

"Fantastic site! I hope everyone will visit and the fear and stigma will be removed once and for all. Thank you for your insight. Very welcoming feel the instant you enter..." Kimberly

DEDICATION

This book is dedicated to my mother and superwoman, Tina Quarles-Gulley, who passed away in June 2013 with stage four breast cancer. I want to thank her for taking the time to become more aware of my *mental illness*, supporting my many endeavors, and for her unconditional love for me and our family.

To the many other parents who lost loved ones to mental illness: may you be strengthened and encouraged knowing that you did the best you could do while they were here. May you continue to be a blessing to them by sharing what you have learned from your experience with others whose lives are currently being affected by mental illness through your powerful testimonies.

To my peers living with mental illness: stay encouraged, for there is always life after diagnosis. Be strong and do not let self-doubt, or *anyone*, discourage you from pursuing your dreams.

What's on My Mind? A Collection of Blog Entries from Overcoming Schizophrenia, Volume 1

Publisher's Note: This book is not intended as a substitute for the medical advice of physicians. The reader should regularly consult a physician about his/her health and particularly with regard to any symptoms that may require diagnosis or medical attention.

ISBN-10: 1494923009
ISBN-13: 978-1494923006

Printed in the United States of America
First edition, first printing: March 2014
Second edition, second printing: April 2014

August 15, 2013

My Version of Hope— A Poem

By Ashley Smith

I feel a better me is yet to come,

No more naive decisions that make me feel dumb.

Limitless opportunities are on the way,

I believe I know what I want and how not to stray.

I see myself as the individual I long to be— free, confident, and classy,

My experiences cannot stop me,

Not schizophrenia and depression nor anxiety.

Because ingrained in me is an overcomer of adversity.

Now I understand how to strive in my recovery,

But I cannot take all the credit when it took a caring party.

I give thanks to my treatment team, family and peers,

Including those online that opened up about their fears.

And I will never overlook my miracle from above,

Forever recovering and living a life I am proud of.

My faith keeps me going as did my mom.

And now that she is gone, for others, I will remain strong.

Within my spirit hope shed its light,

Now I aspire to share the fight.

Join me as I dare to put myself out there,

And overcome the stigma that we bear.

Hold them accountable,

Oh yes, for the lies and propaganda that so freely is told,

Together we can contribute to the solution,

I urge you, to continue to speak, write, and demolish the confusion.

ARTHOR'S NOTE

All the events in this book are true. I collected several blog entries to share my story, and made minor changes. Also, I have omitted the names of the bloggers who commented on my blog to protect their privacy. This book should not replace the advice of a physician. I strongly encourage you to consult a doctor for any decisions and actions taken to diagnosis and treat mental illness.

Over the course of recovery my perspective about treatment changes from strongly believing in medication into being an advocate for whatever professional services helps my peers and their families. My evolution on treatment is the result of familiarity with people who use diverse coping skills, and have differing backgrounds in rehabilitation.

People living with schizophrenia, or any mental illness, are challenged every day by their recovery and the stigma. We should not judge what we do not understand, instead value the lived experience of my peers.

CONTENTS

ACKNOWLEDGMENTS

Thank you Father God for blessing me, and turning my bleak situation into a positive experience! First, I'd like to give a huge shot out to my *Overcoming Schizophrenia* blog readers and Embracing My Mind, Inc. fans, your encouragement and feedback helps me, thank you for supporting my recovery.

To my loving and supportive family— Valyncia Smith, Carlys Smith, and Clarence Gulley, your involvement in my recovery is dear to me. And to my niece and son who gives me joy, thank you. I love you and I hope to make you proud!

I want to give a warm shout out to Rev. Melody Favor for helping me make this book happen. I appreciate your guidance, wisdom, and love in encouraging me to press forward with this book. I've learned so much from you, thank you!

I want to express a special thanks to my support system, these individuals are close to me and they always go above and beyond what I ask of them, and I am grateful to have them in my life—

Jumel Lewis, Eric Fergerson, and Regina Holloway. Jay, you know me best. I want to extend a huge thanks to you for giving me the most joyful moments of my life, and for truly accepting all of me. You will always have a special place in my heart, and I thank you. Eric, I appreciate your ongoing support in all that I am trying to accomplish. I value your ideas and friendship. Regina, your support for me and my son are touching, I will always appreciate you for that.

I want to recognize and to thank NAMI Georgia for giving me the opportunity to help reduce stigma in different capacities, and to serve as a state trainer and board member. I am sending a lot of love to the NAMI Georgia staff, volunteers, and members- to my fellow board of directors, peers, family members, and supporters. Finally, to the many individuals that I've had the pleasure to partner with, to train, and who've personally reached out to me, thank you.

To my advisor, mentor, and supporters who've given me hope and encouragement: Mona Terrell, Selina Beene, Donna Bullard, Delora Quarterman, Princess Brown, Cathryn Coone McCrary, Kenya Phillips, Jacquelyn Hill-Brown, Jennifer Ayers-Moore, and Corey Jones. Special thanks to Christina Bruni for reviewing this book and for writing the foreword. Chris, I treasure your advocacy and peer support. Much love goes to all, thank you.

FOREWORD

By Christina Bruni

I'm privileged to have met Ashley at the premiere of the Janssen video: *Living with Schizophrenia: A Call for Hope and Recovery.* There, I interviewed her for a special feature article for *SZ* Magazine and reported on the film at my second job. I'm the Health Guide for HealthCentral's schizophrenia community at healthcentral.com/schizophrenia in addition to working as a librarian.

At HealthCentral, I write news articles, profiles on peers living with this illness, and hot topic columns about strategies to live life well in recovery. I've been a loyal reader of Ashley's blog, *Overcoming Schizophrenia*, since its start. I was most impressed by her quick embrace of her God-given role as an advocate for peers. She was called to take up compassionate action to use her experiences living with schizophrenia to help others get help, choose recovery, and not to ever give up hope; and to stay in the treatment that works to give them a good life. Ashley's story is living proof that a person's life can get better after they have a breakdown.

Her blog book, *What's on My Mind?* is the best of its kind, and should be a required reading. This book is a great starting point if one needs to seek help or are newly diagnosed. It is also helpful if you're a family member of a loved one with schizophrenia, a romantic partner to one of us, or a provider seeking hope for their patients to recover. Finally, this book can be for anyone curious about the truth of what it's like to live with schizophrenia.

I know it's possible to have what I've called in my own blog a *magnificent* life even though one has schizophrenia, bipolar, or another mental health challenge. I talk to you from lived experience because I've been in remission from schizophrenia for over 21 years. In the fall of 1987, I got the right help within twenty-four hours. The medication I started to take in the hospital stopped the symptoms within three weeks.

I am the Health Guide at HealthCentral going on eight years, and I'm honored to write this foreword because I too have experience living successfully with schizophrenia. I obtained a Masters in Library and Information Science in June 2000, and I live in my co-op apartment.

It's important to me to contribute to Ashley's book because all too often stigma prevents people from being open and honest about their trials living with this illness. I'm confident when I tell you that Ashley and I are not the exception: thousands of other people successfully live with schizophrenia. Her book gives hope to everyone struggling in silence that the pain is not in vain and there's a light at the end of the tunnel.

The benefit of Ashley's first book is that it's organized in the format of an *In Our Own Voice* presentation with sections focused on aspects of recovery that she would talk about in her real-life public speaking engagements. Her optimism shines throughout. The book starts with "Dark Days" and leads up to "Successes, Hopes and Dreams." I'm impressed more than anything by Ashley's own words in the Introduction: "I accepted my illness, and decided to live."

Today, more than ever, with the right treatment and support, an individual can manage their illness, and the dark days can turn into good days. An individual can have a better life after they get diagnosed more than you could ever imagine. Thank you, Ashley, for sharing your life and experiences with us. I have great interest in the next installment.

Christina Bruni, Health Guide
Author of *Left of the Dial* (memoir), and a mental health self-help book, both forthcoming.
Brooklyn, New York
www.christinabruni.com

*****

PREFACE

My name is Ashley Smith and I want to share my story with you about how I am managing my illness and life. You may be familiar with my blog, *Overcoming Schizophrenia*, which I created in 2008. If so, you have a better understanding of my experience with schizophrenia and of me in general-way to go! In fact, *What's on My Mind? A Collection of Blog Entries from Overcoming Schizophrenia*, Volume 1 is only the beginning.

Although my story is about living with schizophrenia it can easily help, support, and encourage anyone living with a mental illness. However, it can also give insight to loved ones and students wanting to learn more about people experiencing such conditions in recovery.

I believe my story will change an individual's perception about people living with schizophrenia. My hope is that you will come to view yourself, or other people living with the illness, in a more positive way, because overcoming schizophrenia, or any other kind of mental illness, takes hard work!

Please disregard all the scary stories and depressing prognosis you may have heard about people living with this condition, because you do not know *my* story. I am an individual with many aspects: I am an African American, woman, parent, educator, mentor, and an advocate. With that said, I use my blog as a tool to help open dialogue about schizophrenia to challenge people's perspectives. Moreover, reading about my experiences with schizophrenia will undoubtedly:

- Change your perspective on the way you view people living with schizophrenia for the better
- Inspire peers to seek professional treatment, whatever that may look like for them
- Show you how God turned my discouraging situation into my promising career and purpose

I do not claim to be qualified to give advice about treatment on schizophrenia. Therefore, do not use this book as a means to make your mental health decisions. However, I am an expert on my own experience. With that said, I decided to compile some of my blog entries to share my testimony in a quick read.

*****

My sister, Valyncia, encouraged me to start blogging after I returned home to Atlanta. I titled my blog, "Overcoming Schizophrenia" because I viewed my recovery in a positive way as opposed to a significant struggle, for many reasons including: the support I get from my family, my treatment team, and my fight to overcome the illness. The initial intention of the blog was to be used as my personal outlet and therapy to collect thoughts, gather information, and to monitor my experiences with schizophrenia.

I became accepted into the blogging world within the mental health community, and my experience online turned into a phenomenon that forever changed my life for the better. A variety of individuals and groups discovered me and my story through the *Overcoming Schizophrenia* blog, and they reached out to me. Now my blog is easily found on the Internet. Lastly, I encourage you to check out my blog for the most current information on my recovery journey at http://overcomingschizophrenia.blogspot.com.

*****

INTRODUCTION

"The most frightening realization *after* the encounter was discovering that these feelings and thoughts were fabricated in my mind and mine only..." (Overcoming Schizophrenia blog).

How would you react if you learned your mind was disoriented and what you believed to be true was not? Welcome to the start of my recovery.

I am living with schizophrenia. I choose to share my experience with the illness to offer insight to others by utilizing my blog, "Overcoming Schizophrenia." In fact, this book is a collection of select entries from my *Overcoming Schizophrenia* blog.

I've been in recovery since 2007. I am overcoming this illness with the support of my family, treatment team, peers, and my faith in

God. I am a Certified Peer Specialist (CPS) in Atlanta, Georgia. In other words, I am a peer counselor that supports other people living in recovery with their mental illness-I share my testimony, support their goals, and help advocate for their needs.

I became comfortable sharing my diagnosis with the world as a result of my exposure to different programs, projects, and advocacy groups such as the National Alliance on Mental Illness (NAMI). NAMI educated me on different mental illnesses, helped build my self-confidence in order to publicly share my story, and strengthened the essence of my peer support.

Currently, I am a state trainer for the NAMI program "In Our Own Voice" (IOOV). In fact, this volume is structured into the IOOV format; however it does not substitute for an IOOV presentation. I selected blog entries that identify with each section of the presentation and organized them into chapters:

1. Dark Days
2. Acceptance
3. Treatment
4. Coping Skills
5. Successes, Hopes, and Dreams

First, the **"Dark Days"** section set the foundation of my personal experience and understanding of schizophrenia. In the past, I struggled with bizarre thoughts, intense emotions, and confusion from living with my untreated mental illness, which I reflect on in this section. My testimony revisits the difficult moments that led to my diagnosis.

In spite of the Dark Days, I accepted my illness and decided to live! **"Acceptance"** goes into detail about how I came to accept my illness through various people, situations, and my faith, which gives me strength and hope to move forward in my life.

The **"Treatment"** chapter informs the reader of the processes I went through to get well again. However, it does not specify medications used to treat my disorder *intentionally*, to respect the IOOV presentation guidelines. Refraining from disclosure of the specific medications I use to treat my disorder is absent, because I do not want to promote brand names. I do not want to mislead anyone into believing my medication will work for them because it may not-everyone responds differently to medication.

The **"Coping Skills"** chapter provides information on my struggles, and the skills I use to help me cope with the illness. This chapter shares ways that I have managed my symptoms in addition to my doctor's own recommendations.

Finally, the **"Successes, Hopes, and Dreams"** chapter shares some of my projects and accomplishments. This chapter details my efforts to promote anti-stigma messages, tell memorable events, and to share my passion for advocacy.

Although the information in this book is organized according to the IOOV format, and facilitates my story, it does not make up a live presentation. The experiences described in this book do not share every detail of my life in recovery.

Furthermore, some blog entries are accompanied by "anonymous blogger" comments to give a real life perspective. Occasionally, I will ask the reader questions and provide space for them to write answers. These questions and comments may help facilitate discussions, especially for peers living with a diagnosis, family members, educators and students, and also any others who want insight into schizophrenia.

I hope this book will inspire peers to get into some form of professional treatment whether that include traditional or alternative practices. I want to encourage family members to be hopeful that their loved one will get well. Finally, my ambition for this book is to offer insight, to change perspectives, and to reduce stigma. This book does not substitute professional guidance and treatment.

*****

CHAPTER 1

DARK DAYS

The mind is so amazing and powerful, it is a terrible thing to lose... How has your dark days turned into good days?

September 8, 2008

My Nervous Breakdown

A little over a year ago my psychotic experience led me to steal a military pickup truck. I took the truck in hopes of escaping the "demons." I thought everybody was out to get me. This incident led to five months confinement in jail and also in a California state hospital. While there, health professionals were able to diagnose me with schizophrenia.

At first I thought I was in hell, but then I thought being in jail was a hoax. Fortunately, my family was very supportive. They visited me, wrote emails, and collected bail money. However, my sickness would not allow anyone to get too close. The illness had taken over.

In my mind I wanted to see my family, but I felt blocked. I denied visits, mail, and would not call anyone. Whenever I got mail I threw it away without opening it. I told my mother not to put any money towards my bail. My family chose not to bail me out, because they did not know how to help. Instead, they postponed bail because they wanted me to get medical attention-I did not have health insurance.

I was not the same person as I used to be. I did not engage in Bible study, or conversation with others in jail. Eventually, I became catatonic, and would not move, literally. I stayed in one position for hours, staff later told me. Initially I was practicing being still to please God, similar to a practice like fasting. However, the routine took control of me. I think the voices also contributed to my repetition. Before I became catatonic, I chose not speak, shower, or eat. The psychiatric unit in jail sent me to the emergency room *three* times to put an IV in me to keep me hydrated and alive!

I could not tolerate group settings, so I isolated. I was uncomfortable around others. They gave me medicine to help calm down, and then I was able to endure groups of people. With treatment the negative symptoms disappeared and I gradually returned to my old self. However, I would have to deal with court issues, social phobia, and anxiety due to my realization, and shock of being in jail.

In spite of my illness, my family never left me behind. They continued to visit me and find information about my illness. I am thankful for my family, and the medical teams who treated me. Fortunately, the judge had empathy for me, and instead of being charged with a felony, my charges were reduced to a misdemeanor.

My Question for You:

Have you ever lost your ability to function? If so, how did you overcome it?

Your Answer:

"While I have never experienced what you went through I did have a breakdown about two years ago. I felt that I had failed at everything, and my life was a mess. I was depressed and didn't realize it, my family couldn't help me because I shut them out. I felt like I was drowning. I don't talk about that time very much now. I still feel pain and hurt from some things that happened to me. I believe that for the grace of God I would've been dead had I not been able to change and get help.

It really lifts my spirits to read your blog and see your change. Someone else said that it takes courage, and that's very true, you never know when someone will need to read your words, keep it up!" Anonymous blogger

"I am self-diagnosed with schizophrenia, because I have most of the symptoms but have never been to a psychiatrists for a diagnosis. Nobody knows about it except me. I recently learned that there are different categories of schizophrenia. Anyway, I have gotten much better now just by reading the Bible as it is the Word of God that brings healing to our souls. Just want to encourage you to continue the medication and to read the Bible daily. God will see you through this trial. God bless you." Anonymous blogger

*****

September 21, 2008

Detrimentally In Denial

"I am *not* sick!" I shouted at Erwin, the jail nurse.

"Yes, you are sick." He said. "We had to take you to the emergency room three times to stick an IV in you because you were not eating. Yesterday, the guard had to drag you in your chair back to your room because you would not get up. You are sick," Erwin said, which was followed by my silence. "Will you please take your medicine now?"

There were so many incidents where I was being difficult, such as this that I am finally able to put together. In one incidence I refused to put on my shoes even though I had to go to court. The guards did not understand my condition. They resulted to strapping me down to a wheelchair because I would not walk, and I went to court barefoot that day. I learned from my mom that this was so unexpected that it caused an uproar in the courtroom. This probably does not happen much, but even the district attorney, whose job it was to slam me, remained silent and accepted whatever recommendations my attorney gave. A psychological evaluation was ordered, which I failed.

My mother later told me that there was so much compassion for me in the courtroom that day from the judge, the bailiff, to the court clerk, and again, the district attorney. This was the court hearing that determined I was incompetent to stand trial, and the request for penal code 1370 carried. My mother, grandfather, and aunt shared this emotional moment in court. Well, it was emotional for them, but I was emotionally removed. My mother also told me that during this court hearing I sat in the wheelchair, still. I did not move or lift my head, *nothing*. In fact, she believed that if a bee would have stung me, I wouldn't have even flinched. Before, most people believed I was on drugs. However, my mother told them that I was anti-drugs, and "No!" that was *not* the situation.

Reading a Bible scripture which instructed a person to stay still and to "worship God," contributed to my irrational determination to practice being still, literally. I did not take care of myself because of my illogical reasoning, which was a symptom of schizophrenia. Moreover, I did not eat because I thought the jail staff were working together to try to poison me with food. Other times I thought I saw bugs in my food. I stopped showering, because I thought someone tampered with my soap and that it would burn my skin.

"Ashley, you need someone to represent you, and whatever problems you have with me, we have to deal with that later. But right now you're out there by yourself, you need to let me help you," my mother pleaded with me. I responded with a blank expression on my face, and ignored my mother's advice, *again*.

Finally, I was court-ordered to take medication. Whenever I refused to take medication a group of guards bombarded me. To me they looked like the SWAT team, and they held me down while the nurse gave me an injection. This routine went on for quite a while before I gave in and took the oral form of my medication. I later learned that my mother and family encouraged my attorney to request the judge to mandate medication compliance, because I was slipping away. Today, I accept I have a serious mental illness, and that it requires medication in order to maintain recovery for me.

I am using this blog to heal, network, and to reach out to others with similar illnesses. I never want to go back to where I was mentally, emotionally, and physically. If there is anyone debating, or neglecting treatment, *please* cooperate with your doctor and act on their recommendations.

Where I am right now, versus where I was is like night and day. Through my understanding of not being completely healed, I realize recovery is an ongoing process. I would not be able to do the things I am doing right now without treatment.

There are so many horror tales I could share with you and maybe I will as we go along. But, nevertheless, understand that I am so thankful for treatment.

"I'm so glad that you're sharing your story with others. It provides the much needed hope that is sometimes hard to find." Anonymous blogger

"This is a wonderful tool for others struggling with this illness. Best of luck to you." Anonymous blogger

*****

January 14, 2009

Schizophrenia & Voices: The Ugly Side

Schizophrenia is a complex mental illness that can alter a person's judgment and emotions. The illness affects one percent of the population in the United States. For males it usually begins around age 15, and for females around age 25. However, I showed symptoms at age 20 or perhaps younger.

I had jumbled thoughts, and heard loud voices demanding me to say and do things. None of what the voices said made any sense. In fact, there were multiple voices. The voices were discouraging, and mean- sometimes they laughed at me. The illness made me have intense moments. I also had a hard time following what people had to say in conversations. Schizophrenia can make an individual become an ugly person... unless one manages it. The following events happened to me while I was in jail:

I woke up one night because I couldn't sleep, the voices were bothering me: "Get up, flush the toilets," A voice commanded.

To quiet the voices, I started flushing all of the toilets. Even though I woke up my fellow inmates, I continued flushing the toilets. A woman "Sh" me and grabbed me by the arm to take me back to my bunk.

"Get the vacuum cleaner," demanded another voice.

I got up again, this time to use the vacuum cleaner, but not for its intended use. I hit the camera on the ceiling with it.

"What are you doing?" Another woman asked me.

No response.

"If you don't go to sleep I will call the guards on you!" the inmate warned.

Another time, during a visit with my sister, the voice said, "she isn't your sister."

"Lynci, who was your childhood friend?" I asked her, trying to decipher if she was my sister or not.

"Why are you asking me this, Ashley?" My sister asked.

"I just want to know," I said.

My sister replied, "Christina..."

Schizophrenia can make an individual turn into an ugly person. The illness alters logic and takes away everything that is important to the individual such as family. I denied visits from my mother and father, and well, *everyone.*

"Tell her you don't want to see her again," the voice commanded me while I was on a visit with my mother.

I had a blank stare that scared my mother, as I looked into her eyes and told her: "I never want to see you again."

"Why, Ashley?" she replied in an upset tone.

"She isn't your friend! She kept your father away from you," the voice said.

"Because you hurt people," I said. "You took my father away from me. You took my boyfriend away from me," I said, and abruptly left my seat to stand next to the door to return to my cell.

Later...

"Ashley, can I get you to sign this release form so that your mother can see your medical records?" asked Elaine, the social worker.

"Say no," a voice said.

"No!" I shouted.

Elaine returned to my mother in the front office and told my mother I said no.

"Will you please ask her again," my mother pleaded.

"Ashley, can I give your mother permission to see your medical records?" Elaine asked.

"No!" The voice shouted.

"No means No, b#!*h! Get out of my face, b#!*h!" I shouted banging on the door with my balled fists.

One day the guard had to drag me in my chair back to my cell because I would not follow orders to get up. I became catatonic, not moving a muscle for hours. In the beginning, I recited scriptures: *"Trust in the Lord with all your heart, lean not on your understanding... Be doers of the Word not hearers only... Before I formed in the womb I knew you, I ordained you a prophet to the nations."*

Eventually, I had jumbled thoughts or no thoughts at all. I remember doctors coming into my room to check on me. They would move my arm and ask if it hurts, but I did not respond. I chose to be mute...

"She's evil, don't talk to her," the voice said.

I was selective with who I spoke to. Whenever I did speak it was limited, such as "yes" and "no."

"The nurse said you don't talk to anyone. So they put us together so that maybe you can talk to me," a woman told me.

"Oh." I said. The nurses' tactics did not work and eventually I did not speak at all.

"Ashley, it is time for you to take your medication," the nurse said.

"No!" I replied. I was very uncooperative.

"Come on, it will make you feel better," the nurse pleaded.
"I don't want to." I replied.

"Okay, well we will just have to call the guards to help me give you a shot," the nurse replied. "Don't make me do this..."

Shortly after, several guards came charging at me and pressed down on my arms and legs. I couldn't move, I was stuck! The nurse gave me a shot. This routine went on for a few days, until I finally got tired of getting shots, and I gave in to taking the oral form of the medication.

Accordingly, the voices went away as a result of the medication. I started moving around again, and getting involved in conversations. Although schizophrenia is a difficult illness, there is hope that one will get well again through medication and therapy. Moreover, my mother and I are close again.

"For me personally, I miss my voices...they complimented me, talked to me, told me who I was, told me about my life history, inspired and overall me a creative person. Without them, I am a mess...how can I possibly get them back?" Anonymous blogger

My sister has it ... She refuse to take her medicine because it make her sleepy all the time... She still live with us but she fights with us over delusional things and that makes everyone hate her... Can you tell me what kind of medicine you are on and does it work and make the voices go away, because the pills she was on doesn't work it just make her less active." Anonymous blogger

*****

February 9, 2009

Schizophrenia: Disorganized Thinking

A part of cognitive symptoms can include disorganized thinking, or specifically for me, "loose associations," and poor concentration. By "loose associations," I mean connecting situations that have nothing to do with each other. I was delusional, I created stories and believed them to be true without any justification. Also, it was hard for me to stay focused and to complete tasks such as homework or job related assignments. Despite the many symptoms I experienced, I did not know I developed schizophrenia.

An example of one of my delusions or created stories was a taxi-cab driver told me to "stay out of trouble," this statement led me to believe he was following me or watching me. Another example of my delusions and loose associations that I experienced took place while I was working for a relative. One day I collected a piece of mail addressed from New Jersey. In the past, my ex-boyfriend frequently visited New Jersey. I created a story that led me to believe my mother went to New Jersey and drove my ex-boyfriend away from me. I accused my mother of taking my ex away from me, and also my father. Despite the fact that my parents divorced when I was a baby.

It would take me hours to complete simple assignments at work and school that I could usually fulfill in a speedy manner prior to the onset of schizophrenia. I tried to do my homework despite the unknown symptoms by taking naps and breaks, working on other projects, or participating in study groups. One day at work I got embarrassed, because it took me all day to write and complete a couple of paragraphs.

Disorganized thinking is also a subtype of schizophrenia. It can include: racing thoughts, poor speech, making up words, delusions, and having a hard time completing basic tasks such as showering. I also struggled with the bathing part, because I thought someone had tampered with my soap and thought it would burn my skin.

"Going through a paranoid episode myself as part of my bipolar disorder I can relate to this post. It was a terrifying experience for me. I thought the whole world hated me and the people of my town were gossiping about me. I had all sorts of other bizarre thoughts. Thank God my doctor was able to help me through this." Anonymous blogger

"From my experience most schizophrenics experience at least some paranoia, but in paranoid schizophrenia the "delusions" are more fixed, so that they can be told as a story. Rather than just paranoid ideation that comes and goes. I'm schizoaffective but my schizophrenic symptoms are more focused around hallucinations and "voices" than delusions. I have been paranoid, but most of the paranoia was fleeting. I don't remember holding on to any "delusion" for more than a day... My friend has paranoid schizophrenia and when he was ill he thought he was going back to ancient Rome to fight the gladiators. His "delusions" are grandiose rather than persecutory, yet he's still labelled "paranoid"... weird, huh?" Anonymous blogger

*****

February 14, 2009

Paranoid Schizophrenia

Paranoid schizophrenia is a subtype of schizophrenia. It consists of paranoid characteristics such as persecution delusions, thoughts that others are following you, and the belief that others are trying to poison you or harm you. I was diagnosed with this form of schizophrenia.

At the time, I believed my family was against me. I thought my family had contacted friends and told them bad things about me. I believed a relative drugged me and that this led me to commit a crime. In reality, I took a military pickup truck as a reaction to my irrational thinking and psychosis. In addition to that, I thought this relative also tapped my cell phone and had a device in my phone that monitored my whereabouts.

I thought peers and professors were conspiring against me. Once, I told a friend: "I could *feel* people gossiping about me." She looked at me like I was crazy and told me nobody was gossiping about me.

At one point, I thought the neighbors were spying on me and giving reports back to my family. What they would report, I have no idea-I had a life, but it wasn't *that* interesting, being a college student. In fact, I confronted the neighbor and told them not to spy on me, so now this incident embarrasses me.

While walking to the store one day I thought I saw a shadow pass me-it was an evil spirit, I thought. (I thought I was a prophet and could decipher good spirits from evil spirits in people). I saw a man following me and got scared. I went into a nearby grocery store and waited till he left. When I left the store I went directly into a nearby fast food restaurant, because I saw the strange man again. I was so scared I asked a complete stranger to give me a ride home, the man I asked was a bus driver. He did not show much concern because he referred me to a nearby bus stop that he said runs frequently. Only recently, I realized this was another hallucination.

"I thought I was Jesus too. It's funny how many of us think we're Jesus. There can't be that many Jesus's! I also have had all the other types of delusional thought processes you describe, and some of them, I still have on occasion, even years after starting medications." Anonymous blogger

"Yeah, I thought I had the gift of seeing 'shadow people' but there were out to kill me. I was also convinced that aliens were putting thoughts and dreams into my head." Anonymous blogger

*****

March 10, 2009

Schizophrenia: Bizarre Behavior

Part of having schizophrenia can include irrational behavior and disorganized thinking when untreated. Before I learned I developed adult onset schizophrenia I had some strange beliefs.

For instance, I questioned family members, to determine if they were my relatives or impostures. I believed they were impostures when they did not answer my questions the way I wanted them to. Where my actual relative went, I did not know.

As I asked these questions I had a blank stare that scared my family: "Who was your childhood friend," I asked my sister..."What high school graduation gift did you give me," I asked my grandmother."..."What did I write on your Mother's Day Card? ...Was it taped or sealed?" I asked my mother..."What shop did you take me to before we went to the zoo a few years ago," I asked my uncle. These questions seemed minor or mediocre, and of no significance, but they were very important to me.

"Where are your glasses? Where is your Bible? Why haven't you been answering my calls," my aunt asked me. (I usually carried my Bible everywhere I went). "I lost them," I replied.

The truth is I left my cell phone at a smoothie shop because I believed my aunt placed a tracking device in it, however, where I was going was no big secret, but I felt violated. I left my glasses in the bathroom, in order to disguise myself from the people following me, but there was no one *actually* following me. I remember being scared at the time and not having any relief from whatever action I took. These were just some of the bizarre things I did, but there is a lot more that I plan to share with you soon.

Now, reflecting on these experiences I recognize how bizarre these incidents were. I realize I was delusional. I am glad there is medication to help overcome the symptoms of schizophrenia. Today I do not have delusions or a lot of symptoms from my illness because of the medication. The intention of this entry is to offer awareness. Although there is no cure for schizophrenia, there is treatment to help reduce the symptoms.

If you are a caregiver, friend, or parent of an individual living with schizophrenia and notice strange behavior you should keep a record of it and share this information with a health care professional. Also, keep hope alive that that individual will get better!

"Your symptoms are so similar to my brother's. He currently questions if my parents are his parents or if we are his siblings. It is a little hard to take but I know this symptom will fade as he gets better. One thing I notice is that he finds comfort (when is completely psychotic) by going to church. My mom told me he has sat in the same pew for almost 6 hours one time. I couldn't believe it. But I think he found peace there. We were raised Catholic so maybe going to church was a place he remembered as calm and peaceful, away from the world." Anonymous blogger

"I've had schizophrenia since 2003. I was obsessed with religion too. I thought I have become a prophet and my hallucinations are messages from God, because of that my hallucinations were scared and very important for me. This was going on for eight months, after that I sought medical help which after three years became very successful." Anonymous blogger

*****

April 12, 2011

Lack of Trust: A Byproduct of My Mental Illness

In this entry, I'll share my experiences with schizophrenia in regard to feeling unable to trust others, having paranoia, and isolating.... I remember experiences with my undiagnosed schizophrenia where I felt uneasy because of lack of trust in others. In the past, isolation was a *giant* bullying me around.

Sometimes my mind would take me to a place of fear, hurt, and an unsettling spirit, which started with what seemed like a strange look, or a different feeling around certain people; in reality it was another symptom of my undiagnosed illness, paranoia. Paranoia went rampant and dictated my life before and during my crisis, or "psychotic break." These experiences led me to act out and to go jail, which accordingly led to my forced treatment, and to receive a diagnosis of schizophrenia in 2007.

In other words, my illness created enemies in my mind. For instance, I believed my aunt was against me, and I felt like she wanted me to fail. Eventually I thought she was conspiring to harm me. She never said anything to imply these thoughts and feelings of distrust. My illness attacked those closest to me. I felt like there were barriers or issues between us, when in reality there were not. My paranoia and lack of trust grew against other members of my family, friends, and ultimately the world.

One day I had a revelation that everyone was against me, because I was special or had special abilities. I needed to escape! I quit my job, cashed my last check, packed my bag and left the house in hopes of renting a room in a nearby neighborhood. When the room for rent idea failed, I wanted to leave the state and go back home to Atlanta.

However, because my symptoms were severe I ended up in jail after taking a military pickup truck from the airport. After my family filed a missing person's report, and discovered I was in jail they visited me. Instead of being happy to see them, I was skeptical. I believed they were impostures, and did not trust them so I was hesitant to speak.

I felt alone, trapped, and timid. I thought someone had done something to my family. Therefore, I questioned them before I had an open discussion. I asked distinct questions, for instance, I asked my grandparents what gifts they brought me for my high school graduation. Whenever a relative got a question wrong I believed they were impostures and I felt very uncomfortable and suspicious.

Later, I was angry with my family because I thought they did offended me. I do not remember why I was so upset. My illness made me distant and skeptical over anything and everything. While in jail, I remember people telling me the date, but I did not believe them. Instead of believing someone's word about the date, I thought God was sending me messages and symbols through milk cartoons.

Eventually, the nurses in the psychiatric unit in jail gave me pills for my mental illness. I refused the medicine because I did not understand I was experiencing a psychotic break. After they forcefully medicated me, or I gave in and took the medication, I was educated about my illness in a California state hospital. Soon afterwards I yearned for family and friends again.

After I went back home I had to learn to overcome isolation. I *wanted* to have friends, I *wanted* to get out of the house, and I *wanted* to learn more about my illness. I started attending therapist-led support groups at the center where I received treatment. I went to all the groups they offered, which was about three a week. And I started rebuilding relationships. As a result, I started volunteering and I eventually went back to school.

I must emphasize I am still learning this process of wellbeing, it is NOT an overnight recovery plan. I consider my recovery an ongoing treatment plan that includes: support groups, ongoing support from family and peers, and medication compliance.

I share these experiences to promote awareness and to also emphasize the importance of trust. I want to promote hope and recovery because I believe they go hand in hand and are possible.

If you have a mental illness I encourage you to find someone you can trust so they can help advocate your needs. If you are a family member or friend of someone living with mental illness it is important to gain or to keep their trust. I suggest you keep an open mind to bizarre experiences and beliefs; journal and encourage treatment, any sort of treatment (therapy, medication, holistic approaches, etc.).

"Hello Ashley, I'm a student in an Occupational Therapy Assistant program and I have been studying about individuals who suffer from schizophrenia, and your blog provides a great deal of insight. I especially love the sentence where you say overcoming this is NOT an overnight recovery plan. This is so true! I have learned in class that it's just like you say, a community effort and lots of support from family and friends to overcome this mental illness. Also, I was reading in one of your previous blogs that you still attend support groups and take advantage of an ACT program. This is so important for others to know because as I have been learning in class, overcoming schizophrenia is an ongoing process that has to be dealt with daily. Another thing you said was very intriguing and is a perfect example of taking one's religion and culture into consideration when deciding if a person is really delusional or just really religious. I'm referring to when you stated that you didn't believe the dates people were telling you were correct because you thought God was sending you the correct date, and it wasn't what everyone else was saying. I do believe that everything happens for a reason, and it appears as though you getting arrested was actually a good thing. I checked out your website. Nice job! It has provided me and my classmates with a great deal of insight. Thanks. I don't know you, but by reading your story I am so proud of you! Keep up the good work!" Anonymous blogger

*****

December 5, 2011

From the Terrors of Psychosis
To Hope & A Better Life

Experiencing psychosis is an experience I will never forget. In short, *psychosis* is when an individual cannot distinguish reality. I endured a psychotic experience at the age of 20, almost five years ago, and I still remember the terrors of the illness. I was diagnosed with *paranoid* schizophrenia in 2007.

The manifestation of the illness dominated my livelihood whenever I was suspicious, confused, forgetful, irritable, distant, irrational, and hearing criticizing voices. In my mind, everyone was envious of me because I had *godly* talents. I thought I could read people's minds and understand them, and sometimes they could read my mind as well. I rationalized these strange beliefs by my faith in God and the miracles of the Bible. I believed I was on a mission for God and eventually thought I was Jesus Christ. I felt like I was being persecuted again when I was arrested for the crime I committed while not in my right state of mind. The bizarre thoughts increased.

While in jail, I thought a relative was playing a prank on me, and I did not know I was incarcerated for a while. Still institutionalized, I began to believe authorities experimented on me and impregnated me by giving me a shot while I was asleep. Then I went on a prayer fast. I remember reading a scripture in the Bible that said to remain still and to worship God, and so that is what I did for hours throughout the day. Eventually, jail staff admitted me into the psychiatric ward in the jail, because I was catatonic and not moving for extended periods of time. This is a glimpse of some of the bizarre beliefs I had, but I could share a multitude of other thoughts, feelings, and emotions I recall from my experience with the illness at its worst.

The most frightening realization *after* the encounter was discovering that these feelings and thoughts were fabricated in my mind, and mine only; the people I thought were against me were not obsessed with me at all and did not want any harm to come to me. I remember slowly putting the truth together while writing in my diary and "second-guessing" myself. I discussed symptoms with my doctor, and learned more about my illness in a state hospital. In fact, I cried after piecing together some of my encounters which were real to me, but not a reality for others. I think schizophrenia can be devastating to the individual living with it, as well as for their family, if they do not cling to hope and faith.

My doctor at the state hospital gave me a lot of hope. He said I could go back to college and live a normal life as long as I did two things: 1) take my medication regularly and 2) to manage my stress. I have not gone off my medication, I continue to find ways to cope with stress such as writing and communicating my needs with others, and I have not experienced psychosis since my diagnosis in 2007.

I reminiscence about the times I was not well on this blog because I made it, and I believe other people living with mental illness can too with the right treatment, support, diligence, and faith. If you or someone you know is struggling with a mental health concern, seek professional guidance and continue to provide them with support.

My hope is that people will view schizophrenia as a medical condition that can improve with treatment, support, and the right attitude. My objective is to reduce stigma, change perceptions, and to open dialogue about mental health concerns. I hope that my story encourages a change in the way people view individuals with these health conditions, and will know that the illness can be managed.

"Pieces of your story resonate with me as well. People speak of naked reality, but naked unreality was what I had to fight against." Anonymous blogger

"Thank you so much for sharing your story so candidly. My father has bipolar I and experienced psychosis many times. So many people do not understand..." Anonymous blogger

"Psychosis was one of the scariest things I ever went through too." Anonymous blogger

*****

CHAPTER 2

ACCEPTANCE

Life is full of obstacles, but there will be a major challenge that a person can either accept, and endure, or deny and struggle. Is accepting mental illness the beginning of recovery?

December 29, 2010

Mental Health Recovery To Me

Yesterday, in group we had a discussion about what recovery means? How do organizations define it? And what tips can we suggest to help an individual reach recovery? I heard various understandings of recovery: change, growth, and to restore what was taken, etc. In addition to getting everyone's opinion on the meaning of recovery, we read SAMHSA's 10 Fundamental Components of Recovery.

My definition of recovery is focused on action. First and foremost, recovery to me is accepting my diagnosis and taking ownership of my wellbeing by seeking treatment and support. My recovery involves treatment planning with my health care providers. It also involves speaking up about my needs and asking questions. In other words, it is about self-advocacy.

Recovery is accepting change and learning the *new* Ashley. That is being real with self and capabilities by revising my needs and goals. For example, the "new Ashley" is aware of her limitations as a result of the illness; I understand that I should *not* work or go to college full time for the *moment* until I reach another phase in my recovery, which is possible!

My recovery plan includes sharing my knowledge with others and educating myself about mental health. In addition to that it is about volunteering and performing outreach to help reduce stigma and to promote awareness.

At this point in my life, I love my recovery! Now, I am open about my diagnosis. I am comfortable with the progress I have made, however, I am continuing to strive to improve. I am hopeful that I will achieve my goals despite living with this illness.

In my experience recovery has helped me to mature. It teaches me some of the lessons of life that I would otherwise not understand

34

unless I went through an event as intense and emotional as my mental illness.

For instance, I learned that I am not immune to a lot of things. I would have never thought I would encounter mental illness and experienced its ups and downs such as the bizarre thoughts, incarceration, therapy; and the whole recovery process.

For me, recovery required a lot of support from doctors, therapists, social workers, case managers, family, and peers. I am thankful for the strong foundation I experienced, and also for the outpatient treatment program and housing arrangement, the group therapy, and for NAMI (the National Alliance on Mental Illness).

Finally, I do *not* believe recovery comes with a time limit... To me, recovery does *not* equal perfection, or is problem free. In my opinion, recovery does *not* mean a person is "cured" of the illness. Instead, recovery means managing the mental illness, which is an ongoing process that demands a lot of attention and support. However, I do believe the level of progress in one's recovery depends on the information gathered, support, and involvement in treatment.

My Question for You:

Whether you are a family member or a person living with a diagnosis how has recovery changed your life? What does recovery mean to you?

Your Answer:

*****

August 29, 2011

Changing With My Recovery

It is amazing how much my recovery has changed. I can remember a time in my recovery where my goal was to socialize with people because I felt distant and isolated. Now, I regularly engage in conversations with peers and others. It's great to see how my recovery progresses and goals change. I have many goals that I update. For example, one of my short-term goals was to complete the Certified Peer Specialist training, and after three years of trying to get into the training I can check that off my list!

Another goal was to live independently. As I mentioned in another blog entry, I enrolled into a county housing program that allowed me to live in a personal care home. This experience was empowering because I made this decision, and felt in control of my life again. My current housing situation enabled me to live alone and to make decisions for myself. My hope for peers living with schizophrenia is to be empowered by their decision making and accomplishments.

I believe it is important to take part in managing my recovery. Self-direction is also critical to my satisfaction in life. Now I think recovery is about being able to do what I want and need to do to be content.

Despite the diagnosis, I believe we should all have the opportunity and privilege to make decisions, and to advocate for ourselves. Schizophrenia can seem like a scary illness, but it is doable-I am proof!

My Question for You:

Are you willing to change with your recovery? For family members and caregivers: are you willing to allow your loved one to make their own decisions?

Your Answer:

"It means getting along with people. It means having God in my life." Anonymous blogger

"Of course I am willing to change! That's the whole point! And yes congratulations Ashley for becoming a CPS and for having a home, where you are your own boss. I am very happy for you!" Anonymous blogger

*****

February 25, 2012

A Recipe For Acceptance & Wellbeing With Schizophrenia

The NAMI-Athens, Ohio radio station interviewed me, and I wrote this for their followers:

For me, understanding my mental health condition enables me to move forward in my recovery. A combination of acceptance, support, treatment, and faith, motivates me to strive for well-being, which is a sense of normalcy in spite of my preexisting medical concern.

How am I overcoming schizophrenia? My journey is an ongoing process that I will continue to thrive on not only for myself, but for my family and peers. Now, I will share with you how I have mastered my recovery of mental health and how I am living a quality life.

Since my diagnosis of a serious mental illness in 2007, I have learned how to cope with my condition and how to keep a good attitude no matter how other individuals living with or without a mental health challenge view the concern. Getting to this level of comfort was not easy. In short, I have battled housing discrimination, social judgment, and self-stigma, among misconceptions of the community made known through uneducated comments and beliefs in response to my recovery, experience, and the illness in general.

Although accepting my illness came in my initial stages of treatment I would not have been well again had it not been for the support of my treatment team, family, peers, and faith in God. For me, getting support required having an open mind, being willing to share personal experiences, and to offer support to others. Support from a range of connections was crucial to me because I needed a cheerleader or a supporter on my side to keep hope alive and to instill the idea that recovery was possible.

Although I am on medication to help treat my mental illness, I understand there are alternative treatments available and unique ways to reach peace and well-being with mental illness. I am an advocate for whatever healthy coping mechanism works. The underlying factor that helped me accept my condition was my faith in God to help me overcome schizophrenia, my new purpose to support peers, and to help them realize there is life after a difficult challenge with mental illness.

In fact, when I was diagnosed in the hospital a few years ago, my mother told me that I will be an evangelist, and share my testimony about how I overcame schizophrenia. Back then, I did not understand how it would happen, but my faith led me to believe that the idea was possible, which gave me hope.

I was featured in a documentary, along with two individuals living with schizophrenia, that was produced by Janssen Pharmaceuticals Inc. called, *Living with Schizophrenia: A Call for Hope and Recovery*. I have personally traveled to and spoke to communities in Canada and across the United States. My story was also presented on CNN and BET.com among several other media channels. Now, I share my recovery experience with law enforcement and facilitate workshops to support peers and family members affected by mental health.

My hope is that schizophrenia will be viewed as a manageable medical condition and that understanding will flourish and ultimately reduce widespread misconceptions and myths. It is an honor to share my life with schizophrenia in our community and abroad. I plan to write a book about my experiences and to manage a wellness center for individuals affected by mental health.

"Ashley, Congratulations on your ongoing recovery with schizophrenia. I am happy that you have been able to get all the support from your family and community. As a current psychology graduate student and a student worker at NAMI, I know how hard it is for people to live with mental illness and be able to fight the self-stigmas and community stigmas. I think that speaking out about your experiences is so empowering not only for yourself but for others who struggle with the mental illness. In addition, I love that NAMI provides the crisis intervention trainings for police officers and glad to hear that you are able to be a part of it. More professionals in our community should be educated about mental illness so that people do not have to experience housing discrimination, or get targeted by law enforcement. Best wishes to you and all or your endeavors!" Anonymous blogger

*****

CHAPTER 3

TREATMENT

Finding the right medication demands trial and error... If you take medication, or don't, how successful have you been with managing your condition?

February 26, 2009

Good Doctor, Bad Doctor

One of my readers shared an upsetting story with me. They told me their relative's doctor lacked faith in recovery and gave a negative viewpoint. The doctor told the family that their relative will never improve, and they should not get their hopes up. This is one of the worse things a doctor could say. I think doctors should have high standards for their practice. I wonder why people are in those professions if they don't think their patient has a chance, or if they have no faith in their own work.

I just want to make one point clear: it is a myth that someone with schizophrenia cannot recover, they just have not found the right treatment. However, I encourage peers and their supporters to seek treatment and to keep hope alive! A lot of my readers living with schizophrenia or another mental illness are success stories.

I had a doctor that I do not think *really* cared about her work. She was not there for me when I needed her. I complained to her about the restlessness, a side effect of my medication. I had trouble sleeping at night because I felt like I had to stay in motion. I made my requests known to my doctor to change my medication, because I did not like the side effects. Fortunately, there was another doctor on site that was available too and she gave me more medication to help me cope with the side effects.

The other doctor managed my treatment when I was not well and catatonic. I believe any person should have a say in their treatment; it's their right! I suggested a medication that I read about it in an article about bipolar disorder. I thought I was bipolar because nobody told me what my illness was they just forced me to take medication. My doctor did not consider my request because she assumed I would slip into another catatonic state. Accordingly, I did not share concerns with my doctor, because I did not feel like I had a choice. I requested the other doctor whenever the opportunity arose.

Despite this experience, I had an awesome experience working with my state hospital doctor. I'll call him "Dr. W." He switched my medication to the one I wanted right when I got into his care (and I did not have a relapse). The medication I was initially put on made me at risk for developing diabetes, which is also prevalent in my family. I guess this was carelessness of my first doctor.

Dr. W went beyond his duty and arranged a meeting with my mother and treatment team so that she would have a better understanding of my illness. This time I signed the form my mother to have access to my information. Their meeting was held during the time of the major fires in southern California in 2007.

My mom had a hard time getting there because most of the roads were blocked, shut down without notice. Dr. W actually helped my mother to navigate the trip in order to meet with her and to discuss my condition. My state hospital doctor and social worker, Katie, stayed until my mother arrived.

My doctor scheduled this meeting in advance, and told my mother to come prepared with questions. My mother, stepfather, and sister created a list of questions for my recovery. My doctor gave my mother a lot of important information about my illness, the scope of various medications, and signs to look for in case of a relapse. Dr. W also told her there was most definitely hope for me. My mother told me he said he wanted me to succeed!

I respect Dr. W because he listened to my concerns and cared, which showed in the way he spoke to his patients. He was the one that gave me the news that I had schizophrenia; he wasn't like the previous doctor I mentioned above that shoved medicine down my throat and expected me to understand my illness without warning. Dr. W made an analogy between schizophrenia and diabetes to explain that treatments will be needed, since there is no cure for schizophrenia or diabetes.

Finally, there are good doctors and there are bad doctors-that's life, but nobody should have to suffer the burden of a bad doctor. My advice to you if you are facing a challenge, such as my reader, where your doctor lacks faith in your recovery is to change that doctor *immediately*! And if you can't change doctors, then find a good support group that you can share your concerns with and get more information about your condition.

Schizophrenia, or any kind of medical ailment, needs to be nurtured. For example, people with diabetes like my mother, need to monitor their diabetes, have a good diet, and in some cases take medication. Likewise, people with schizophrenia need to take medication to control their symptoms, just like people with diabetes need to control their sugar levels.

As I may have mentioned previously and I will keep on mentioning this, recovery demands medication compliance, support, and a positive outlook. There are a lot of places where you can get support, not only from family, but also from organizations such as the National Alliance on Mental Illness or the Schizophrenia Society of Nova Scotia (Canada), and from online support networks such as Health Central.

My Question for You:

Have you ever experienced a bad doctor? How did you handle this and what advice would you give to others in this position?

Your Answer:

"Ugh, I've been dealing with a bad doctor. I have to be in a really good state or mind with him to make my concerns known or he just tries to give me a script and get me out the door. I don't really like him, but don't really want to go through finding another one either.

You're absolutely right, it is a patient right to have a say unless declared otherwise legally. If I'm not in a psychotic state, I get to say NO! If I don't agree, and you have to answer my questions with a direct answer... that's why I'm paying you, for your medical knowledge to make me feel better. Period.

My advice, if you can't get a new doctor is to keep a bulleted journal between appointments so you don't get flustered in front of the crappy doctor and make all your concerns known or have someone you trust go with you to your appointments as a patient advocate. And most importantly for me, schedule the appointments when you have as much time and as little stress as possible.
Thanks for writing about such an important topic."
Anonymous blogger

*****

January 20, 2011

My Acceptance With Mental Illness

Acceptance to me is when a person recognizes they have a mental illness and then takes ownership of their recovery by meeting the needs of their mental health concern (i.e., medication, therapy, and/or alternative forms of treatment). Acceptance for me did *not* come easy. Now I will share with you how I started receiving treatment, why I initially refused it, and who helped me accept my diagnosis of paranoid schizophrenia.

Initially, I was *forced* into treatment, mandated by a judge to medication compliance. Therefore, whenever I refused to take my medication a group of jail guards would barge into my room, pin me down to the bed, while the nurse administered a shot. We followed this routine for a few days until I gave in and started taking the pills.

In the beginning, I did not take the medication for several reasons: 1) I did not believe I needed them, and nobody told me that I had schizophrenia, they just started giving me medicine one day, 2) I had a history of enduring allergies and other less severe illnesses without medication, and 3) I did not want to let the medication "weaken" my spiritual gifts. In other words, I lacked insight into what was actually happening to me; I was falling apart-I had had a nervous breakdown

49

or psychotic break. I did not see myself failing to take care of personal hygiene, not engaging in activities and in conversation with others (isolation and poverty of speech), or did I notice the fact that I would stay in one position for long periods of time (catatonic).

Growing up, I let colds and allergies fade away on their own. I did not want to be dependent on medication unless it was something more serious like the flu. Lastly, when I noticed a change in my ability to read people's minds or to decipher their good or evil spirit, I felt like the medication was interfering with my God-given talents. When in truth, the medication was bringing me back to reality!

After giving in and taking the medicine, another problem occurred... The SIDE EFFECTS! I would sleep all day, every day. I missed out on group therapy and free time with peers. On top of that I was extremely hungry to the state of *not* being able to focus, can you imagine?!

Moreover, a downside to another medication was lack of sleep. I could not sleep because I felt compelled to move about-this was restless legs syndrome. After experiencing this, I did not want to take my medication. (This is one of many reasons why some of my peers living with a mental illness do not want to take medication.) I complained to staff about my side effect (restless legs) but with no avail until I caught the attention of another doctor. In the meantime, nurses bribed me into taking my medicine with candy and juice.

Finally, I took a medication that controlled the symptoms with a more tolerable outcome... *stiffness*. I did not feel stiff, however, medical staff would ask me how I felt and would move my limbs and ask me if I felt any discomfort because, well, I walked like a "robot!" This is what my peers called me behind my back, a friend told me.

Then, the *talk*. My doctor told me my official diagnosis— *paranoid schizophrenia*... but wait! I was NOT devastated, because I was blessed with a great doctor. Let me tell you why: he had a passion for helping patients. He explained what the symptoms of schizophrenia were and applied them to my specific situation. He said my illness could explain all the symptoms I was experiencing— the voices, delusions, etc., which made me feel a little better, but *wait*, this is not the only reason why he was a great doctor!

I had a great doctor because he believed in my recovery. He had hope for me! He told me that I can go back to college as long as I manage my stress and take my medication regularly. He said I can lead a normal life as long as I did these things. His confidence in my recovery gave me HOPE that I *can* do it! And now I am... Now I am going to school part-time. I volunteer, and live independently.

If you, or a loved one, is living with a mental illness there is hope. For me, it began with *acceptance*, and trying to meet the demands of my mental illness in order to get well and to stay well. I take my medication as prescribed, participate in a few support groups each week, and stay connected with my support network.

"I'm so glad you had a great doctor! People often hear horror stories about bad doctors and your story about having a good one I think help dispel some of the stigma and fear surrounding getting the proper help." Anonymous blogger

"I have a great doctor too. It's a blessing. I had very similar problems with accepting the illness and with the side effects. How familiar! Thanks for sharing!" Anonymous blogger

*****

August 19, 2011

Who Is In Control of My Recovery?

Are we listening? Are we listening to the one in control of recovery? Who is in control of recovery? Is it our doctors? Our family members and friends?

For a brief time, I did not have choices in my recovery. My life was limited by the California state jail system. In fact, I had my choice to deny medication taken from me. I was court-ordered to medication compliance, which was encouraged by my family. However, I am thankful my family advocated for medication compliance because it ultimately saved my life! I recognized this only after I was treated and educated about schizophrenia.

When I was not well a few years ago, I believed I was a victim of conspiracy. I thought someone in my family was playing a prank on me and took me to an enclosed facility with different routines (jail). I believed others were against me and were working together to poison me and to spy on me. I felt like my life was in danger, and that I had reason to feel uneasy and suspicious. As a result, I did not speak much, eat, or shower, because I feared someone tampered with my soap and believed it would burn my skin. All the while I thought I was okay, and did not take medication.

After refusing medication one day, a group of guards along with a nurse barged into my space, restrained me to my bed and gave me a shot. I refused to take medication several times after that and we went through the forced medication routine regularly. Eventually, I complied with the nurse's request and took the pills because I did not want to receive another shot. The nurses did not tell me why I was forced to take the pills, what my mental health condition was, or the type of medication.

Soon I felt some uncomfortable side effects to these pills and did not want to take them. The nurses knew why I did not want to take the medication, but bribed me with candy and beverages to take them anyway. Now, I wonder why the nurses did not advocate for me and take my concerns to my doctor, or maybe they did with no further instruction, I don't know.

The pills interfered with my sleep and made me feel excited and jittery. I complained to my doctor with no solution. Eventually, I found an alternative route to have my concerns met. I talked to another doctor after my doctor left. This helped; the other doctor gave me another medication to relieve the side effects.

One day, I asked the nurse for information on my medication. And I learned of the type of medication I was on and other additional information. While reading a magazine I came across an advertisement for medication, and it listed some of my experiences as symptoms. I took this advertisement to my doctor to request a medication change. My doctor said no because it was not in my best interest to switch medication for several reasons, including risk of destabilization. I felt like I was not being heard and like I did not have any control over my recovery.

This feeling of lack of control in my recovery changed when I went to the state hospital. For the first time, a doctor asked me what I wanted. They gave me options and I made a choice, which we agreed upon. Moreover, they suggested I get off the medication my other doctor put me on because of my family's medical history. I felt like my opinion mattered and that I was in control of my recovery.

Since that hospital visit, I continue to play an active role in my recovery. After I was released from the correctional facility and the hospital, I joined a county program that offered housing, among other services. My mother enabled me to make the decision to move into a group home, commonly called "independent living," or personal care home, despite her concerns. I was in control of my own recovery and life.

My treatment team helped me go back to college, because it was *my* goal. When I moved back to Atlanta with family, they suggested activities, but they did not force me to do anything I was not ready for. Eventually, I got frustrated with limited social support from the community and made the decision to go to the support groups offered at my treatment center to meet people, and to make friends.

I am in control of my recovery and life. I say that because while treatment teams, family, and others supported me with options, but the final decision was mine. Now I live alone, I am in college, and I lead support groups.

Self-direction in a person's life is essential to recovery. I experienced empowerment by being able to make decisions, and I want my peers to have the option to do the same. I am an advocate for my peers by sharing my personal recovery story, and by sharing resources and information to support them and to also help reduce stigma.

This week, I completed the Georgia Certified Peer Specialist (CPS) training. The priority of a CPS is to give the individual living with a diagnosis a voice. A CPS listens to the individual and advocates for them to their treatment team and others. The role of a CPS is a growing movement that is established in several states across the United States.

Finally, Embracing My Mind, Inc., a mental health organization that that I started, offers peer support and will have educational recovery support groups that is open to the public. The group will meet at the East Point Library in East Point, Georgia starting Thursday, September 8, 2011. Please go to the website for additional information. The objective of *Embracing My Mind, Inc.* is to reduce stigma, change perceptions, and to promote awareness and hope.

"I've been diagnosed with schizophrenia as well. Being paranoid, afraid and cautious has led to several unjust experiences at the hands of "professionals." I know *now* I'm in control of my recovery but wish whole heartedly to advocate for others with the schizophrenia diagnosis— where to start? I've seen far too many people ignored. Delusions…. Whether it can even be called as such… are traumatic. I had amnesia at a young age over a very horrible memory. Top those with medication for symptoms in a terrified countenance… how can an individual call it "Paranoid?" It's *real.* In that the doctors, nurses and other staff take matters into their own hands and ignore the suffering the patient is going through. Meds didn't help me… not for years. It took an act of God to keep me alive. Well, thanks, just venting and looking for one who could relate." Anonymous blogger

*****

Ashley Smith

September 14, 2012

Fear To Openness About Medication

I am concerned that I may be slipping into depression that will get worse if untreated.

Prior to the birth of my child I never had a problem with depression, but as my body changed so did my hormones and my susceptibility to depression. A few months ago I was diagnosed with postpartum depression and at the time I knew I needed extra support from my treatment team. I knew I needed to focus on my mental health because my anxiety level was high, it became difficult to concentrate, and I felt extremely overwhelmed and afraid my schizophrenia would rear its ugly head and try to destroy my recovery accomplishments. I spoke with my therapist who contacted my doctor and let him know I was coming in the next morning as a *walk-in*. I did come back the following morning and we tweaked my medication.

Now, it's hard to focus and to carry out minor assignments, sometimes I feel anxious for no reason, I am extremely tired and sleep more than usual, and I feel like I am on a downward spiral. I have a lot of personal stresses that may contribute to these new feelings.

Lately, I have been participating in more support groups than before. I guess my subconscious was aware of my need for additional support before I noticed I needed it. I go to two therapist-led support groups a week and co-facilitate one self-help group. The meetings really help me because I am able to get a lot of information from my therapist and peers. For example, I asked my therapist what the common side effects are for antidepressants, and how long does it take the body to respond to them.

In the past, my doctor prescribed antidepressant medication that I filled, but did not take because I did not know enough about the medication and believed the depression rose. Now that I understand what the common side effects are and how long it could take my body to respond to it, I am more open to taking it with the new information I learned from my therapist. Moreover, my doctor said to start the antidepressant medication if I felt I needed them. I need them. I will start taking them today in addition to the medication I am already taking.

If you or someone you know is in need of treatment, but is afraid of getting treatment for whatever reason, I encourage you to get educated about treatment by asking a healthcare provider questions.

"Hi Ashley, I understand how you feel. For a short while, I had to take an anti-depressant. It's actually quite common that people with schizophrenia need to take an anti-depressant as part of their medication routine.

I hope you can start to feel better. You are brave and wise to consider every possible option for maintaining wellness. Yet you are also smart to get your questions answered about the effects of the drug and any side effects.

I found that taking the anti-depressant was much better than lying in bed all day. Whatever a person with schizophrenia needs to do to stay in the game of life, I can understand this. Keep the faith, there is always hope." Anonymous blogger

*****

May 12, 2013

Medication Compliance: Challenges & Coping Skills

In general, I take one anti-psychotic and one anti-depressant medication once in the morning time. Taking medication can be challenging for me especially if I forget to take the medication in the morning. In the past, I used to skip my dose of medication if I forgot to take it in the morning but I would not take it in the late evening, because I did not notice the effect it had on me the following days. However, I do not do that anymore; my body and mind has changed over the years and I must take my medication *every* single day to avoid the consequences, which include my partner taking notice and the discomfort I feel in that, and the risk of my many symptoms of paranoid schizophrenia flaring up.

Now, I recognize a change in me whenever I miss a day of medication; for me, I lose concentration or eye contact with people and whatever is in front of me. This tendency makes me feel very uncomfortable because I generally keep eye contact with people.

I understand there are a lot of routines I could do to remember to take my medication such as keep a pill container for every day of the week, to set my alarm, or to take my medicine when I do a daily practice like to brush my teeth, and I have tried a few routines. Now that I know there are ill effects if I do not take my medicine daily, I am even more prone to remember to take it in order to avoid my ramifications of embarrassment and discomfort in front of my partner and others, or worse, disorientation caused by my mental illness.

Another reminder of why I need to stay compliant on my medication is my past experience of jail time, my family's concern during that delicate situation, and the accomplishments I have made since my diagnosis. Yes, taking medication is a life-long challenge for me but it is necessary for me to manage my severe mental illness and to take charge of my life!

My Question for You:

Have you noticed any changes when you do not take your medication?

If you are a family member, do you notice when your relative is not taking their medication? If so, what are their initial signs?

Your Answer:

"I have schizoaffective disorder, PTSD, and SAD. I am on an anti-psychotic, mood stabilizer and anti-anxiety med. I notice I sweat a lot when I forget my medication. I also become very anxious and suffer from more catastrophic thinking than usual. I can also become irritable. Other times, I don't suffer any psychiatric symptoms at all, but I just sweat a lot and my heart pounds.

I try my best to keep up on my medication. I have an electronic med reminder with an alarm. You can fill it up with up to nine consecutive days of doses. It really helps me, as when I just had a regular pill box, I would forget my doses a lot. I feel better these days…." Anonymous blogger

"I have been diagnosed with several different things but one is schizoaffective disorder. If I didn't take my medicine or if I miss a dosage then my whole body will react to that missed dosage. It's like my lips will begin to tingle and I just feel out of sorts (hard to explain). But right now my voices have been extremely loud and telling me not to take them because they are poison." Anonymous blogger

*****

February 6, 2013

Learning More About My Symptoms & Diagnosis

A few weeks ago I asked the question: "Mania or Something Else?" Well, I got an answer to my question, plus some!

I visited my doctor a couple of weeks ago and he confirmed I was experiencing "hypo-mania," which is what a fellow blogger assumed I was experiencing. To my understanding, hypo-mania is similar to mania; however, it is not as extreme where incidents lead to harsh consequences like arrests.

When I was in this state of mind I was obsessed with working on my laptop, I blogged more frequently than usual, and I felt like I was on an upward swing, which was a little unusual; this lasted for about a week and then quickly spiraled down into irritability. After sharing how I was feeling with my doctor, we tweaked my medication.

I am glad I have a better understanding of myself-now I know how to identify hypo-mania moments!

However, my previous discussion with my doctor led to another in-depth discussion with him-I shared previous moments of hypo-mania, which as a result made him believe I may be living with *schizoaffective* disorder, which is a combination of bipolar disorder and schizophrenia. The incident that put me into jail a few years ago may have been the result of my experience with mania.

To explain how my illness led to jail: I took a sitting pickup truck with the keys in it from the airport. I believed it was a blessing from God and my escape to get back home across the country, and was my emotional refuge. I was not thinking rationally, because I heard a lot of criticizing voices and had strange beliefs like I was Jesus Christ, and I thought everyone was demon-possessed. I even had an out-of-body experience in which I felt something, or another spirit, was controlling my body and driving the truck. Later I discovered the pickup truck was a military truck and I was facing felony charges. Fortunately, I was diagnosed with schizophrenia, which woke me up to the fact that these symptoms were not going away-after receiving treatment, and learning more about my diagnosis.

Now, a few years later I am wondering whether I have an accurate diagnosis... I do not think my doctor changed my diagnosis; however, it is something to think about.

My Question for You:

Do you believe you or your loved one have an accurate diagnosis? Why or why not?

Your Answer:

"I think I am diagnosed correctly but it took ten years which is a long time not to receive the correct treatment. I had many, many doctors and only a few knew the proper therapy for OCD and ERP therapy is pretty essential to treating OCD. I have no doctor now in the area where I live who does ERP and my doctor only prescribes medication sadly." Anonymous blogger

"I am glad that you have some answers now. And I am also glad that you have been able to turn your life around following the time in jail.

It took me years to get the right diagnosis and treatment, partly because I didn't understand that I was ill and partly because I was never taken seriously by doctors and psychiatrists. I started having symptoms in 2006 and was finally diagnosed in 2011. I have psychosis and anxiety, but officially am only diagnosed with psychosis. Whether this will change in the future I don't know." Anonymous blogger

"Thank you for your blog article. I am diagnosed schizoaffective with PTSD and anxiety. After an initial diagnosis of major depression, it took me 8 years to get out of denial that I did not have a spiritual problem (I heard voices, sensed spirits, etc.) but a bon a fide mental illness. As with you, my faith sustains me and helps to make my life more positive despite having a devastating illness. As of today, I am still hesitant to disclose my illness to those not my close friends and family members because of the stigma and ignorance, but I am getting bolder." Anonymous blogger

*****

CHAPTER 4

COPING SKILLS

Coping with a mental illness demands more than medication. Is medication the most important tool for recovery?

January 18, 2011

Tonight's Support Group Meeting

I just got back from a NAMI support group. It was a very good meeting we covered a lot information related to coping with our mental health, our attitude toward stigma. Afterward, I felt energized, uplifted, and empowered like the way church makes me feel it was a very good meeting. I really enjoyed the meeting with my friends, who are also in recovery from different mental illnesses. I look forward to next week's meeting!

*****

June 7, 2012

Overcoming Ongoing Challenges

There will be ups and downs living with any mental illness. Recently, I have experienced some bad days, which has concerned me very much because I usually do not have a lot of bad days to the extent that I need to take a step back and to regroup, emotionally, mentally, and physically.

Stress makes my illness flare up or worsen, I know this by experience; however, fortunately I usually understand how to cope with the stresses of my life by discussing my concerns with family and friends, writing, listening to music, or walking- I handle my stress like other people handle theirs who are either living with or without a mental health diagnosis.

In the past, my stresses of college and finances led my symptoms to escalate to psychosis-where I heard voices that other people did not hear, saw individuals that did not exist, experienced confusion, anxiety, irritability, irrational thinking, racing thoughts, etc. etc.

A few weeks ago, I experienced some bad *days*. In the beginning, I felt jittery, anxious, and then exhausted and irritable. One morning I had a lot to do; however, it took me three hours to get out of

69

bed despite the aid of the snooze button and alarm, which I pressed and set a few times because I felt extremely overwhelmed and tired. I did not make my first meeting and almost was late to the second meeting that morning. The warning sign that warned me that something was wrong was not only the long morning in bed, but also the high-level of anxiety, which reminded me of my physical state during the most difficult time in my life, five years ago, when my life went out of control-in my mind, and in reality because of my undiagnosed mental illness.

This feeling of anxiety frightened me, and I thought to myself that I have come too far to let my diagnosis pull the rug from underneath me now. I have accomplished a lot since my diagnosis, for my schizophrenia to flare up and to steal my joy like it did a few years ago. I knew I needed to take a break, and *fast*!

Prior to the bad days, my stress built up. I recently gave birth to my son, which that alone impacted my mood and hormones like it would for any other new mother, living with or without a mental health diagnosis; my personal relationship has also been especially challenging with our little one to adjust to. I had a lot of events to either host or to participate in, a weekend training out of town, to train peers in a two-day training, to manage a workshop, and to attend a conference- all within a month's time, among my regular daily life stresses for myself and family. So, I had a lot things going on in my life at the time my bad days tried to dominate my livelihood.

I did what worked for me in the past to cope with the stress, and to recuperate, by discussing my challenges with close family and friends. Accordingly, we decided I should seek professional support *immediately*, and to stay in the respite center for clarity and a fast resolution to overcome my uneasiness and exhaustion.

I called my mental health clinic and requested to speak to my therapist, which enabled me to talk to her that same day. As a result of our conversation I made an appointment to meet with my doctor; however, I went back to the facility the next morning as a walk-in because the appointment was a week too far out for me. I shared information with my mental health doctor on how I was feeling, what I was doing that may have contributed to my health, and what other medications I tried that previously worked for my concerns. Together, my doctor and I made some adjustments to my medication and made a follow-up appointment for the near future.

To help me cope with these new stresses, I went to a wellness center and interviewed for and requested a respite bed for a couple of nights. A respite bed is a comfortable place for individuals who need to regroup but do not want to go to a hospital and their symptoms have not worsened to the extent that they need to go to a psychiatric hospital.

Accordingly, I made arrangements for my son and then checked into the respite center and stayed there a couple of nights-I would have stayed longer, but I wanted to return home to care for my son, because I missed him. During my stay at the respite bed center I relaxed, ate a lot of snacks, and got a lot of rest.

Analyzing the situation now, I think I alleviated a hospitalization stay by immediately addressing my mental health concerns, by being honest with myself and those that can help, and by seeking professional advice to prevent a crisis. I recognized I needed help and sought help before it spiraled out of control. Now, I do not feel uneasy or anxious! I am thankful for my support network and access to services to help me overcome schizophrenia. I believe that if my peers, who are experiencing bad days, recognize their early warning signs and triggers or experiences that made their symptoms worsen, and then seek professional help, they can prevent a crisis.

I shared this experience with you to let you know I still have challenging moments, despite taking my medication regularly, and I overcome them with support. If you experience some bad days, I hope you will recognize them and seek the support you need to overcome your challenging moments too.

"This is a fantastic post. It really shows how having a support network and a triage plan can make all the difference. I'm sorry you had the tough time, but I'm so glad you were able to get the help and rest you needed. Wow. It is a great example of what it means to really try to take care of ourselves, and treat ourselves well." Anonymous blogger

*****

December 19, 2012

When Coping Isn't Coping Anymore

Since September, I have been busy with business: board meetings, conference calls, and presentations, which are very satisfying. However, I feel like I am working on overload, and it's not a good feeling.

Right now I have a lot on my mind. Lately, I sleep too much, forget too often, and lack motivation to carry out typical house chores, which I have to force myself to do. Over the last couple of days, I took the maximum dose of anxiety medication that was prescribed to me by my doctor and it helped a little. I wrote in my journal, and read a little to relieve my racing thoughts, tension and the feeling of being overwhelmed. However, I still feel uneasy.

I have used most of my coping skills, such as writing, reading, listening to music and cleaning-now I need to talk someone about this because I do not understand what is happening to me. I feel like I am gradually breaking down sometimes, while other times I force myself to do what I need to do, and I do get a lot accomplished. I have a lot to think about: my family, finances, and *life* in general! I am not sure if this is mental health related, or if it is the result of me functioning under a lot of stress. I will seek out help from my therapist either today or tomorrow.

My Question for You:

How do you cope with stress and/or anxiety?

Your Answer:

*****

December 20, 2012

The Plan From When Coping Isn't Coping Anymore

This blog entry is in response to my last, "When Coping isn't Coping Anymore," posted on December 19, 2012.

Recently, I have been under a lot of stress, so I tried my usual coping skills that usually worked for me in the past with dissatisfaction and no relief. Accordingly, I went to speak to my therapist to learn new ways to help me cope with my stress and anxiety. Fortunately, I came after most of the traffic died down in the mental health center, and was able to speak with her.

We came up with a stress management plan. The plan is to set a time frame, or parameters, around the time I spend on the lap top doing business. I will prioritize my work load and take more time out for myself to relax. I plan to try this new way of limiting the time I spend to my business for a week or two.

After talking to my therapist about the many things on my mind, I felt some relief and satisfaction with the stress management plan we created. I feel safe knowing that these feelings are more stress-related than the byproduct of my mental illness, though stress can lead me to experience some symptoms of the schizophrenia.

75

Experiencing what I have with schizophrenia in the past, I do not want to go through that again, and I do my best to take care of myself to help reduce the likelihood of relapse.

"Hi, My stress coping is playing the guitar and tennis. And it is important for me to get more sleep longer." Anonymous blogger

"I'm proud of you for being in tune with your body, humble to ask questions, brave to ask them quickly and strong to put new information into practice immediately. Good job! God bless." Anonymous blogger

"I admire how you dealt with your increasing awareness of feeling stressed. I love how you talked about it so clearly with your therapist and how aware you were of things were getting to be too much. Kudos!

Lately I am trying to tune in better to what I am feeling and thinking, and giving myself permission to set limits. Thank you for being you!!" Anonymous blogger

*****

December 30, 2012

Identifying Triggers

Over the last six months I have been battling depression, anxiety, and feelings of being overwhelmed. My doctor calls it "postpartum depression," resulting from the birth of my child, but I call it "life!" Prior to the birth of my son, I did not have a lot of depression. However, I am not sure if I agree with the postpartum depression diagnosis, because of several other factors that may contribute to my depression and other symptoms around the time of receiving the diagnosis.

I know stress is a major trigger for me, and I am still learning what type of stress is unhealthy for me. Despite life's many stresses, I think I have narrowed my stressors to being criticism from individuals within my support system, arguing, over-productivity, and major life changes to me, like relocation.

Now that I know what stresses me out the most, how will I cope with daily struggles? For one thing, I need to continuously work on my communication with my support network in order to reduce unnecessary misunderstandings and confusion. I think we all can learn something new about mutual communication and cooperation. Furthermore, I should analyze what I am arguing about to see if it is an ongoing concern, and who I am arguing with, to decipher whether that relationship is healthy and worth preserving or not.

Also, I like to stay busy but I understand that overworking myself is dangerous for me because it can set me back, despite all the things I've done for myself and for others. I remember prior to my first concern about depression, I participated in an intense two-day training, facilitated a training soon afterwards, traveled a lot, and applied for another leadership position, all within one month. Although this was positive stress, it was still pressure. I remember feeling like I was over doing it, which I was, and how exhausted and on edge I felt with all that I had done and planned to do in the near future.

Relocation- it doesn't have to be across the country as it was in my past- it could be down the street or to any new environment. I admit I move around a lot-always have growing up-and I make it a bad habit to do so now. As an adult, I justify a move because of convenience and to get more space. These are reasonable excuses; however, because of my mental health concern, I should reevaluate my motives.

My Question for You:

What are your triggers? How do you cope with them?

Your Answer:

*****

January 16, 2013

Learning About Mindfulness

Although I have little understanding of mindfulness, I tried to practice its form of observing in the present moment and deep breathing. A couple of nights ago, I did a brief mindfulness exercise, or my understanding of it. As I was sitting in front of my laptop, I stopped working on it and closed my eyes. I concentrated on the sounds around me; the laptop and refrigerator dominated the sounds of my environment. I took a few deep breaths and I realized I was tired, mentally and physically, so I told myself I needed a break. Therefore, I called it quits, temporarily for the hours while I slept. I know there is more to mindfulness than that so I did some research to have a better understanding of the practice.

I learned that mindfulness is based on Buddhist philosophy and was developed by Jon Kabat-Zinn who is "a famous teacher of mindfulness meditation and founder of the Mindfulness-Based Stress Reduction program at the University of Massachusetts Medical Center."

In fact, his definition of mindfulness: "Mindfulness means paying attention in a particular way; on purpose, in the present moment, and nonjudgmentally." In the beginning, the practice was used to help people with a range of medical problems; however, it is not only for people who have illnesses-it can be used to help improve the quality of life for everyone.

Mindfulness incorporates a range of principles and activities: Acceptance, Breathing, Consciousness, Non-judgmental Attitude, Observation, Present tense, Stretching, Yoga. After studying about mindfulness, I would like to learn to practice it the correct way to take advantage of its full benefit.

My Question for You:

How familiar are you with mindfulness? Are you willing to use the practice?

Your Answer:

*****

August 3, 2013

Coping Takes Work

"Thus also faith by itself, if it does not have works, is dead." James 2:17 NKJV

I agree with this scripture because everything in life demands some effort to get the desired results. Likewise, taking medication to treat mental illness with no coping skills and others support while expecting the illness to go into remission is not the most effective process, for there is no magic pill, mental health recovery takes   work.

Even though my schizophrenia seems to be under control and my depression improved I still struggle and learn new ways to better cope with the condition. Lately, I have been pushing myself to straighten up the house every day and to go outside and enjoy the sun, even if it is only for twenty minutes. I also listen to music and share stresses with family and friends. I think keeping up my appearance and getting sunlight has been the most useful coping skills I practice on a daily basis. I am not where I want to be with my depression right now, but I have hope I will get there soon. Now I plan to continue putting in the work in order to better cope with my depression.

*****

CHAPTER 5

SUCCESSES, HOPES, AND DREAMS

Schizophrenia was my sorrow and fear, however, God turned it into my motivation and qualification to educate others...

How can personal testimonies from individuals who are living with mental illness change perceptions and fight the myths?

January 30, 2010

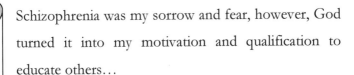

The radio interview went *very* well! Kim Iverson (radio talk show host) and I discussed episodes, her personal experience with mental

illness through her mother, and how family reacts to one suffering an illness.

I shared my story and how I realized something was wrong only after a nurse contemplated with me that I was sick, and told me I was rushed to the emergency room several times because I was not eating, taking care of myself; showering, or even moving! Kim's mother had an episode and Kim was forced to drop out of college to take over her mother's business while she was sick.

The interview was for about seven minutes. I felt really good about sharing my story and the interview overall. Thank you for everyone's support on this event!

And a special thanks goes to Kim Iverson and her radio staff for having me on the show and for allowing me to share my story. Thank you!

*****

February 18, 2011

Messages of Hope

Don't let schizophrenia steal your joy! If you or someone you know is living with schizophrenia or any mental illness there is *hope*.

Schizophrenia is a manageable illness like other medical conditions with treatment and support.

Hope to me is to hear my own voice and only my voice when I am alone. I am thankful that I tried something that manages my hallucinations and other symptoms. I am hopeful that others living with schizophrenia may find the treatment that works for them too. And I am hopeful that society will find solutions to the many complications associated with the cause, or causes of the illness, and to find better treatment, or better yet, a cure for this medical condition!

Someone with schizophrenia can live a "normal" life in recovery. Managing this illness is an on-going process. There is no set time frame for recovery. And, I will say this again, *there is no set time frame for recovery;* everyone is different and may require unique avenues to reach stability despite one's challenging illness.

I am an example of someone successfully managing schizophrenia! I am still in recovery, still putting together the pieces of my past realities or product of symptoms, and I am still learning myself like many other people who may not have a diagnosis.

What helped me in my recovery is treatment, hope from family and health care professionals, and education, education, education! Here are some websites about schizophrenia and other mental illnesses:

- Substance Abuse and Mental Health Services Administration (SAMHSA)
- Schizophrenia and Related Disorders Alliance of America (SARDAA)
- National Alliance for Research on Schizophrenia and Depression (NARSAD)

Yes, schizophrenia scared me, yes, schizophrenia stole meaningful relationships from me, and yes, schizophrenia even had the audacity to take away daily choices from me...but today, I am overcoming schizophrenia, and you can too!

*****

March 24, 2011

NABJ Panel On Schizophrenia Awareness: The Experience

Today I participated on a National Association of Black Journalists (NABJ) panel about schizophrenia awareness in Washington D.C. My fellow panelists included: Judge Arthur Burnett, Sr., Annelle

Primm, M.D., M.P.H., Xavier Amador, PhD, Jennifer Ayers-Moore, and Jennifer Pifer-Bixel, and moderator Vicki Mabrey (and with us in the photograph are some of Janssen's executives). Here is a summary of the panel discussion:

We discussed a range of schizophrenia information: the basics or symptoms, myths, and personal testimonies. More specifically, we mentioned the need for more education and success stories in the media. Additionally, Assertive Community Treatment (A.C.T.) groups were discussed in regard to helping people, who are living with a diagnosis, stay involved in their treatment and to get the necessary resources to move forward in their recovery. "ACT" teams generally consist of a group of health care professionals that assist people in the healing process. Another group that was mentioned to help people stay involved in the community was the Mental Health Courts. Mental Health Courts were developed for people who had encounters with law enforcement or jail system, mental illness, substance abuse, and/or HIV/AIDS, to stay connected to the community.

Religious beliefs and delusions (having false beliefs) was another topic. I shared experiences regarding my faith and how I did not recognize the signs of mental illness because I thought I was spiritually gifted like the people in the Bible. In short, I thought I had the gift of discernment; therefore, I could decipher "evil" spirits and "good" spirits within people with extreme sensitivity. In addition to that, I did not know what a mental illness was, and I did not recognize that I needed support from a professional because I lacked insight.

Some panelists emphasized that support is crucial to a person's recovery as well as treatment, with which I most definitely agree. A member of the panel even stressed that insight into one's illness was not essential to reach a state of wellness, and that relationships are key to recovery.

One barrier to treatment for some members of the Black community were addressed. Some people feel like doctors are not culturally sensitive enough to help them cope. However, more programs are being established to encourage and mentor young Black students to get involved in the medical field in order to develop a medical career in the future. One of the ways the program strives to reduce barriers to treatment is to enhance the growth of more Black medical specialists to help support the needs of the community.

Finally, with the assumption that media perpetuates misconceptions about mental illnesses, panelists encouraged journalists to also bring attention to people overcoming the illness and educating the public about mental health. Yes, in some incidents people living with a diagnosis may be involved in a crime; however, journalists can also educate the public about the facts through success stories.

Overall, I had a wonderful experience serving on the panel alongside influential members and contributors to the mental health field. I felt supported by each member on the panel. I feel honored to have played a role in the panel discussion and to have served on the program alongside my fellow panelists. For more information on the NABJ event visit the website at www.nabj.org.

*****

May 7, 2011

Living With Schizophrenia, Documentary Premiere

The premiere of the documentary, *Living with Schizophrenia: A Call for Hope and Recovery,* was an amazing experience! My personal journey in mental health recovery was one of three stories featured in the documentary.

As a participant in the documentary, I had an opportunity to serve on a panel discussion to share more information about my journey in recovery. The panel discussion was moderated by JC Hayward, and the panelists included Dave, a caregiver, Emily, director of the documentary; myself, as a mentor; Joshua Bell, peer counselor; and Rebecca Phillips, a writer.

The half hour film depicts the lives of three individuals living with schizophrenia. I was united with some of the other individuals who are featured in the film, in addition to the director of the documentary, who also has a personal connection to the illness.

For me, the documentary portrays a message that schizophrenia can be manageable and that people living with this condition can lead a high quality life. I believe this film will help reduce stigma by offering encouragement to people living with a mental health challenge, and also to family members, caregivers, and others. The film was very educational because it addressed some the misconceptions and myths associated with schizophrenia, some treatments, and the symptoms.

The premiere of the documentary took place in Washington D.C. on May 6, 2011. The film, which is funded and produced by Janssen Pharmaceuticals aims to increase awareness, and to reduce fear and stigma.

"Your blog is so reassuring, and the film about schizophrenia is very well done. I think you're brave to out and be so active. I'm recovering, and I hope to reach out to people through my poetry. I am attending a conference soon with my doctor and I will write about it soon." Anonymous blogger

June 4, 2011

NAMI New Jersey 2011 Conference My Experience

Dr. Rebecca Roma and I attended the NAMI New Jersey conference: "Shaping the Future of Mental Healthcare," which took place earlier today. NAMI New Jersey screened the new schizophrenia documentary that we were both featured in called, *Living with Schizophrenia: A Call for Hope and Recovery*. We were accompanied by a few Janssen executives and associates; Janssen funded and produced the documentary. It was a pleasure meeting Dr. Roma because I discovered some of her volunteer work projects and her reason for getting in the medical field, among other interesting conversation.

I had a great experience! I listened to some great speakers and among them was Dr. Robin Eubanks, who had a lot humor, energy, and really got the audience talking-it was very interactive. Also, I was able to get my questions answered in a workshop, "Choices in Recovery," (a Janssen program) about schizophrenia. Overall, having the opportunity to meet Dr. Roma and to be a part a wonderful documentary and the NAMI New Jersey conference was an amazing experience.

*****

June 25, 2011

Sunlight Village
Mental Health Conference

Thank you, Sunlight Village Board, staff, and volunteers! I had a great experience at your mental health conference: "Our Children, Our Future," on Saturday, June 18, 2011. I appreciate all your warm welcomes and support. It is nice to know I have friends in Dayton, Ohio. I would love to work with Sunlight Village again in the future!

At the conference, I delivered the speech, "The Gift of Recovery: A Consumer's Perspective." I shared my personal recovery story from the diagnosis of schizophrenia until the present. I went into detail about my recovery process because I wanted others to understand that recovery is a life-long journey that takes work, persistence, and support. I enjoyed the interaction with the audience.

*****

November 11, 2011

CNN: Human Factor

Recently my story was featured on CNN's Dr. Sanjay Gupta's Human Factor. I feel blessed to have an opportunity to share my experience with diverse communities around the world. I believe it is important to share my mental health condition with the public in order to help reduce stigma. Yes, sharing my mental illness has been a process.

I remember when I started this blog in September 2008 I was unsure about its theme and how much I would disclose. Initially, I did not share my true identity, and now I am very comfortable disclosing to the public about my health condition because I have overcome many medical and social setbacks. I believe this illness can be defeated through treatment, support, faith and hard work.

For individuals and families still struggling with a mental health concern: as you know, there will be many obstacles to reach peace with mental health and to live in recovery; however, there is hope. I remember the stories my mother and family shared with me about their worries and concerns for my well-being during my own battle with schizophrenia. In the beginning, we did not know I was battling mental health. In fact, I thought it was stress and emotional and spiritual battles. However, my condition worsened over time. Therefore, I encourage families to seek professional guidance when debating whether mental health is a factor.

I am so fortunate to have a family of warriors. My mother and relatives stuck by me during my most vulnerable moments. My mother got involved with the National Alliance on Mental Illness (NAMI) and gained a better understanding of my condition by meeting with my treatment team at the state hospital (after I gave consent).

In short, I encourage families to learn as much as they can about mental health challenges and to get involved in a support group to get more resources and support.

Lastly, I had a great experience during the process of producing the CNN Human Factor story. I am so thankful to the CNN team and my communications staff for working so diligently on my story. My experience is one of millions in America, and I am hopeful that we can, "overcome mental illness together!"

*****

September 27, 2013

My Recovery:
Stamped & Approved By Me!

September 2013 is National Recovery Month. *Recovery Month* promotes the societal benefits of prevention, treatment, and recovery for substance use and mental disorders; it celebrates people in recovery; lauds the contributions of treatment and service providers; and promotes the message that recovery in all its forms is possible. *Recovery Month* spreads the positive message that behavioral health is essential to overall health, that prevention works, that treatment is effective, and that people can and do recover.

With proper care and treatment, between 70 and 90 percent of persons with mental illnesses experience a significant reduction of symptoms and an improved quality of life. (National Alliance on Mental Illness, NAMI)

September 2013 also represents my five year anniversary for maintaining this blog, which I started in 2008. At the same time, September is my birthday month, so yay!

As I reflect on my journey of recovery that began in 2007 at the age of 20, I can look back with peace of mind, and joy, to see and experience maturity in recovery. Since my diagnosis of paranoid schizophrenia in a state hospital in the summer of 2007, I have created a new life for myself that is no longer defined by my academic achievements and failures, but by consistent invaluable experiences in the mental health field that has molded my recovery; my involvement in the lives of my peers, advocacy, and in volunteer work.

There is life after diagnosis of mental illness-I am proof! I have accomplished many of my goals, which will continue to change along with my recovery plans and responsibilities. Some of the goals I have made: living independently, obtaining my driver's license again (it was taken from me for the incident I committed that landed me in jail), and becoming a Certified Peer Specialist (after three attempts to get into the training), among other accomplishments. Now I hold a few leadership positions in the mental health community, including board member, mentor, trainer and advocate.

I say all this to emphasize that an individual living with mental illness can fulfill their goals-whatever they are. Therefore, I urge you-whether you are an individual living with severe and persistent mental illness, a family member, educator, or professional, etc., to have hope for a better future for people affected by mental illness because success is defined by the individual and it is attainable. In fact, I have overcome many obstacles, such as not having health insurance, having a fixed income, and being looked down upon because of my mental health condition, but I have endured!

My hope and goal is to finish college, become a homeowner, and to gain full-time employment among many other goals, which I believe I can reach, as long as I maintain consistency in being compliant with my treatment regime, surround myself with like-minded people, and have faith!

Recently, I found myself so stressed and tired at another daily challenge that I had to use self-talk to encourage myself to keep pushing forward. I told myself aloud, "I can do this. I can do this-there are people who are willing to help me. I can do this." And this statement helped me to look at the positive side of situations and to keep going.

*****

CHAPTER 6

FINAL WORDS

An individual living with schizophrenia, or any mental illness, must continue to endure. The reward is recovery and your *life*.

February 6, 2009

Schizophrenia Is Not Caused By Bad Parenting!

The situation that I am about to discuss with you is very personal and a sensitive topic; however, similar things most likely occur in other people's families as well.

After I had my psychotic break, relatives believed my mother was to blame for my illness. They believed I wasn't raised right and my mother's parenting skills were to blame. Although this was a harsh attitude towards my mother, it was another form of denial. Family made accusations, although I was not even raised in the same state as the rest of my family. Once a person has a mental illness, the "who's," "what's," "where's," and "whys" really do not matter. The only thing that should matter is supporting that person back on the right track and moving forward toward recovery.

During my childhood, I always felt loved by my mother. She would call me her "princess," "little queen," "pumpkin pie," or "raccoon." I remember her telling me, "I love you," and exchanging hugs before bedtime. She always had high standards for my sister and me. My mother was very strict-we had a specific routine to follow: do our chores, do our homework, and then play.

Before my illness interrupted my life, I was involved in a lot of activities. My mother still does not understand how I managed to juggle so many activities while I was in school, to this day. I was involved with my college cross country team, part-time job, church, and school. I was very active, an over-achiever having made the Dean's List my freshmen year of college. My family never remotely imagined me having an illness such as schizophrenia.

Accordingly, my family's anger turned towards my mother. She was an easy target because she did not live her life the way other relatives wanted her to. She divorced my father when I was a baby and did not remarry. Neither of my relatives lived a perfect life either, but it was very easy for them to point a finger. This incident caused a lot of friction within my family, which still has not been resolved.

The truth is, nobody is to blame for mental illness. My great grandmother having a mental illness is evidence that the illness started its course before my mother was even born. If you are a victim of being called a bad parent because your child has a mental illness, it is not true, and you are not alone.

There is no known cause for schizophrenia, but it does involve a combination of genetics and environmental factors.

"About three years ago Margaret and I visited my aunt on my fathers' side. Somehow the discussion turned toward my schizoaffective disorder. My aunt said my mom's side of the family is the reason for my "illness." I was aghast. She said look at my brother Mike. Mike is developmentally disabled (DD). I have a nephew is DD too. Later on I talked to mom about it, one of the few times I was allowed to speak of such terrible events. Come to find out I have two first cousins, both on mom's side that had a MI. One I never met. I know there's no known cause for a person's MI. I believe that I was born with schizoaffective and the abuse I suffered as a child and my drug abuse in my teens is what brought it to a head. My psychiatric doctor told it to me like this- The space shuttle that blew up was broken before it launched. I know I was broken before my 1st "break." Whatever the cause, I learned how to cope with it. It wasn't easy, but I feel I turned out pretty good. Recovery is possible. Take your meds, don't drink or do drugs and get real with yourself." Anonymous blogger

"It really helped me to read all the other posts. My son has lived at home for the past 5 years as he felt unwell when working in London. He had a psychotic episode 3 months ago and after coming out of hospital he became suicidal & hung himself after going back to hospital for only 2 days to review meds. I have been looking to blame myself and husband in any way which comes into my head and have been racked with guilt." Anonymous blogger

*****

February 10, 2009

The Path God Chose For Me

I am not upset that I have schizophrenia-this is the life God chose for me. The other day, I was telling my mother I am glad I took a break from school, but I wish I had taken it sooner, so that I could have recognized my illness sooner. She reminded me that everything happens for a reason, and that had I took a break sooner I would not have been able to know my full potential in college and in life. I went to college and got really involved in it through sports, internships, and mentoring peers. I was involved in so many things, school, church, home, friends, family, you name it! She was right-I am glad I took the path I took.

I did not always have schizophrenia, but now that I have it I will work hard to overcome it. I try not to use the word schizophrenic because that identifies the person by their illness and that is not fair. I am Ashley and I have schizophrenia. I will not let it limit my potential or define who I am. I can and will overcome these symptoms with medication, therapy, support, and coping mechanisms.

My mother also reminded me that I used what I learned from my experiences to cope with the side effects of my medication. I was stiff and restless. To control this I exercised, paced, and read the Bible to relax. I also sang hymns and prayed to God.

If you have a mental illness, don't be upset that you have the illness-everybody has imperfections and remember that God does not put more on you than what you can bear.

*****

January 17, 2009

Family Secrets

There is a major difference between gossiping about someone and discussing conditions and/or events within the family. Some people do not want to talk about mental illness because they do not understand it and do not think it is relevant, are in denial, or are embarrassed by it. The fact is schizophrenia is a serious mental disorder that can have detrimental consequences if untreated. Furthermore, not discussing family history can be life threatening: ten percent of the people living schizophrenia will commit suicide. Schizophrenia can also lead a person to isolate themselves from people, to not speak, eat, or even to not take care of personal hygiene.

Some illnesses are hereditary, or places family members at greater risk if there is some background of it; schizophrenia is one of these illnesses. Being aware means you are a step ahead, or proactive, and can look for signs. "Shhhhhh," or pretend like it does not exist? I say "Ouch," to that! Symptoms are not like, "ooooooh" or "psssst psssst guess what," it is knowledge and very important at that! As long as it is the truth, it is not being mean! In fact, I believe it is mean not to share something as important as schizophrenia to your child, spouse, or other member of the family.

Growing up, the only thing my family prepared me for was the risk for diabetes and high blood pressure. Therefore, whenever I filled out the information section of medical history I ignorantly over looked the mental illness box. As a teenager I was athletic, vocal, and ambitious. I made good grades and was involved in high school theater productions. When I went onto college I remained consistent with grades and sports. I never fathomed the notion of having a mental illness.

However, when my life started deteriorating I did not understand what was happening. It totally blew me away!!! It seemed to have come from nowhere, when in fact, it had. I had family history of mental illness, but no one told me.

In order to complete homework assignments, I had to take naps, form study groups, and work on other projects to overcome my lack of attention. Trouble concentrating is another symptom of schizophrenia. As the illness manifested, I lost interest in activities I generally enjoyed, such as Bible study. I stopped eating, speaking, and even showering. Now that was a biggie. My mother used to tell me that if I even got a speck of dirt or dust on me, I'd run to wash it off. I lost interest in life.

When I was diagnosed with schizophrenia my mother was still unaware that we had a history of mental illness in our family. It turns out that my grandaunt had a mental illness; she would accuse her niece of trying to kill her, and accuse the neighbors of spying on her. Similarly, I accused my aunt of trying to harm me, and the neighbors of spying on me. Feelings that others may harm you or are spying on you can be another symptom of schizophrenia.

My family either made jokes about my loved one's behavior or dismissed her illness. But when it happened to me, some of my relatives blamed my mother for my illness. They contributed my illness to a poor upbringing. It is a myth that a poor upbringing can cause schizophrenia. There is no known cause for schizophrenia; it is a combination of genetics, critical moments in brain development, and environmental factors.

To this day, I am still astonished that a relative of mine had a mental illness. When I briefly studied the illness in school, it was so foreign to me, and out of my mind when it came to myself or members of my family. You never know what life may bring you, so be alert and inform yourself about different health issues. Now that I have the illness, I am just glad that I did not have a family of my own, such as a child or spouse to see me in such a mess.

As I research information on schizophrenia, I share that knowledge with my family so they can be aware. I have an 18 month old niece; when she comes of age to develop schizophrenia, I will be alert and know the symptoms if I see them, in order for her to get help if she does develop the illness. However, I hope and pray that she is more fortunate than I and will not have to deal with this illness.

Like all illnesses, it has its ups and downs. Right now I am in the recovery stage and I am taking medication. So far, I am doing very well, and getting better.

Share your family medical history, and be proactive, because one day it may come back to haunt you.

*****

March 7, 2009

What Is Schizophrenia To Me?

This is what schizophrenia is like when untreated: It is a nightmare that you cannot wake up from. The illness causes you to believe that everything is about you: a television program, a song on the radio, a stranger's glare. The illness makes you feel trapped, as if everybody is watching you and trying to harm you, but you can't escape- you are outnumbered.

You cannot eat food because someone is trying to poison you. You cannot take a shower because someone has tampered with the soap and it will burn your skin. You cannot tell your family what is going on because they have been replaced too-they are impostures! You cannot trust your friends because they will run and tell someone your secrets. You know they are gossiping about you and they are out to get you-you can feel it, God has blessed you with special powers that enable you to feel menacing and positive spirits in people; you are sensitive to people's emotions.

Everything is a sign, that truck making a U-turn means you should go back, that taxi cab driver saying, "stay out of trouble," means he is watching you too, and is in on it. The voices discouraging you are people around you-they know everything and are using information against you.

What is schizophrenia? Schizophrenia is a mental illness that corrupts the mind. It makes you believe bizarre things and causes you to act strange as a result of the delusions and hallucinations. The illness alters your thoughts and personality causing you to be distant and secretive, not trusting anyone or letting your guard down, for me, at least.

Schizophrenia is a highly misunderstood, complicated mental illness that many people do not want to talk about and many do not understand. It is disturbing; media portrays it as a characteristic prone to violence. People are afraid of what the person with schizophrenia will do; they don't have any idea what the illness is about except that it is associated with violence. Even church members are confused about the illness-some believe that people with schizophrenia have demonic spirits in them that need to be expelled. Others flat out discriminate against people with schizophrenia in the workplace, within families, and in housing because they simply do not understand the illness.

THIS IS NOT TRUE: people with schizophrenia are upright citizens! They are not prone to violence unless they have a history of violence prior to the onset, which is a very small minority of people with schizophrenia, like the general population. People with schizophrenia are entitled to have lives just like everybody else; they are not filled with demonic spirits. And they deserve to get work and get a home without the hassles. (I have been discriminated against in housing. The potential landlord thought my potential roommate would cause too much stress and suggested that I should not rent a room there.)

However, when treated, you can think clearly and be more conscious to what is going on around you. You are not afraid of the people around you. You can openly voice your thoughts and opinions. You can eat your food in peace and shower with no concern. You can form meaningful relationships again.

*****

April 12, 2012

Soldiers of Recovery

Is mental health a problem or a gift? First, I do not view mental illness as a problem, but a challenge that many individuals can cope with through utilization of one mechanism or another. A problem to me is something that is not getting any attention till it escalates and turns someone's world upside down like in my own experience with schizophrenia a few years ago. In fact, I try to stay open-minded to diverse means of coping with mental illnesses, such as schizophrenia, depression, and bipolar disorder, among many other health conditions dealing with the mind.

Moreover, I am neutral on the support of medication although I personally take advantage of its blessings in my life. To state clearly, I am an advocate for whatever helps my peers cope positively. I have come to understand that there are several positive additions and alternatives to medication, including using one's creativity through arts and crafts, music, writing, and singing. Other possible artsy talents, are taking care of animals, appreciating nature, participating in sports, and volunteering.

I look at my schizophrenia as a gift because it has become my ministry. While I was hospitalized and diagnosed in the state hospital five years ago, my mother told me I would be an evangelist sharing my experience with the community...and that is what I am doing today! I have had the pleasure and opportunity to travel to Canada and several cities in the United States telling others the good, bad and ugly about my recovery story that in turn brings about hope and motivates some individuals to keep pushing on- this is so rewarding to me!

My schizophrenia is also a gift to me, because I am learning more about myself all over again. If I had not experienced something as life changing as schizophrenia, I do not think I would have utilized my talents to support the journey of others in this capacity. Yes, I did not always view my medical condition as a gift; however, now that I am mastering it with the support of family, medication, peers, and my treatment team, and with faith, I feel like I can use my skills to assist other individuals.

Having this medical concern has helped me become less judgmental. Sometimes mental health can go undetected; therefore, it is important not to assume that an individual understands another person's concerns. Although living with a mental illness can be difficult, it can also teach an individual to be a better person-it has for me.

In the past, individuals criticized me for taking a positive view on my mental illness. I think some people were frustrated because of their lack of connections to treatment team, family, and community, which left them wondering how to cope with a serious health condition that was dominating their livelihood. Because some individuals may not see their mental illness as a gift, I want to challenge them to acknowledge the good things that have risen from their experience-maybe the condition showed them who their true friends were. The illness could have enabled them to get more in touch with their true selves through art, for example. Whatever the blessing, I believe more of my peers will see their mental illness as something that can be overcome with adequate supports and hope!

Finally, I look at individuals living with a mental health condition as soldiers of faith, despite their circumstances because they learn to maneuver and to live life with or without medication. I love to see peers living "normal lives" through marriage, career/volunteering, and family life— all of which I value dearly.

I titled this post, "Soldiers of Recovery," because that is what we are— anyone who takes the time to study recovery for themselves or a loved one is a soldier by enduring, learning, and fighting for a better future. I encourage everyone to see the positive outcome of a situation that led them to having setbacks, but have ultimately overcome them!

I appreciate the blessing to be able to mentor others through this blog, Embracing My Mind, and the mental health recovery campaigns including the documentary, *Living with Schizophrenia: A Call for Hope and Recovery*, among several media appearances on my recovery like CNN, BET.com and the Tavis Smiley radio interview. I appreciate you for reading my feelings, thoughts, and experiences related to mental illness... THANK YOU VERY MUCH!

*****

January 5, 2013

Comparisons, Perspectives, & Struggles

Like some of my peers, I have experienced disturbing thoughts, anxiety, and missed doses of medication over the past year. Part of me desires to not rely on medication daily, but I have experienced a glimpse of the consequences, which can be detrimental. I understand how critical it is to stay compliant even more so than a professional can express because I have witnessed the dark side of Ashley, which has been out of control, out of character, and scary.

Some individuals get the wrong impression about me from my blog- some think I handle my illness perfectly or that I am too optimistic when that is far from the situation. I was not diagnosed with all the answers-I, like my peers, have challenges-and it took a lot of practice, effort, and support to get to where I am today. Yes, I am proud of my recovery and have come a long way with the support of treatment and others; however, I have setbacks too, which I articulate here sometimes.

There are a lot of struggles I leave off the blog because it is too personal and complicated to explain. For example, my personal relationships, family life, and family struggles. Because this blog is about my illness, I leave a large part of my life out and focus on a big but also narrow aspect of my life: living with schizophrenia.

I do not like to be compared to because I am not into that, and I believe we should each compare ourselves to our best self. I am grateful that others look up to me, and I love to mentor peers and offer support when asked, but sometimes that puts a lot of pressure on me. I feel pressured to stay well. Yes, I maintain recovery for myself and my family, but I also challenge myself for my peers that look to me for answers.

I could not have managed my schizophrenia without my peers-online, from NAMI meetings, and several other networks. I am not here to dictate anything about anybody-I am sharing my story to let others know some of the experiences a person living with a diagnosis endures and if you can relate, please comment to let our peers learn and understand from each other's experiences.

If you or a family member are struggling-recovery is a process that takes time and commitment. No matter what there will be ups and downs sometimes beyond control. Here is something my doctor told me: 1) manage your stress, and 2) take your medication regularly. It sounds straightforward, but it is a huge task that requires one's full attention.

I understand that many of my peers do not like medication and I don't either, but I take it to maintain control of my mind and actions. However, for some, they have not found the right combination yet; it is trial and error, and I am an advocate for whatever treatment regimen works, whether it is alternative forms of treatment or traditional (medication), just DO IT!!

*****

January 10, 2013

Recovery Partnerships

Recently, I participated in a Certified Peer Specialist (CPS) continuing education workshop to keep my certification, and to learn more information. During the training we identified recovery, our roles and responsibilities, and new Medicaid-billing policies. The training experience reminded me of interactions with mental health professionals and peers who have given me hope.

In short, recovery is a unique learning process that ultimately develops into self-direction. The CPS position is a growing dynamic that has spread across the country and is becoming internationally recognized. The position of a CPS is versatile and flexible in that we are to act as a liaison between mental health staff and peers living with a diagnosis, and to demonstrate life coach abilities by acknowledging strengths within peers, and as a result to support their goals and plans.

Ultimately, the CPS position is to also overcome the mental health system or to help establish a new culture of recovery in that peers living with a diagnosis are self-directed, empowered, and more independent through a combination of peer support, professional assistance, and self-determination. Besides the CPS position, evidence of this new way of treating, recovering, and managing mental illness was practiced several times over the course of my own recovery, which began in 2007.

I am thankful to have had come into contact with the many individuals who supported my recovery in some form. I can vaguely recall the intake process and diagnosis at a California state hospital. But I do remember the intake psychiatrist patiently discussing my medication regimen, tweaking my medications and doses, and giving me options before making changes as opposed to strictly prescribing a medication they thought would help my symptoms without my input. Furthermore, my doctor who diagnosed me with paranoid schizophrenia reassured me that I would be able to move forward in life, despite a permanent medical condition-my most inspiring life-changing realization.

The most intriguing concept I identified with from the training was, "the shared experience," which is the notion that a group of individuals could build a bond, a trusting relationship, and an understanding of each other based on a common experience, such as living with mental illness, and then endure the emotional turmoil, the terrible symptoms, into a fruitful recovery, no matter how unique the journey.

As I reminisce about my journey of living with mental illness, I remember my peers who I came into contact with in the state hospital, clubhouse, support groups, and Certified Peer Specialist training. Engaging in peer support gives me purpose-I remember participating in a WRAP (Wellness Recovery Action Plan) class facilitated by peers and imagining myself also leading recovery discussion groups.

The first time I led a recovery discussion group was in 2009. First, I mentioned to my therapist that I wanted to facilitate our schizophrenia support group. Soon afterwards she spoke with her supervisor and gave me approval to co-facilitate the meeting with her. In the beginning, we would debrief after the meeting and she would identify teaching moments and my strengths. By doing this, I felt empowered, and I encouraged peers to take leadership roles by co-facilitating groups in the mental health center, NAMI meetings, and other networks. I have mentored three peers into leadership positions, and it feels great!

When I attended the CPS training in 2011 I did not know what to expect. However, after the training I felt like I can make a bigger impact on peers' lives with the tools I received during the training. The training was intense, but also empowering. I met several peers who wanted to take on leadership roles in the community and were acting on this goal through the training. The training reinforced my goal to make it my business and career to support peers and families in recovery.

While I was in the state hospital, my mother told me that I would be an evangelist one day-sharing my story about how I made it through with schizophrenia, but I did not know it would become my purpose. Now I embrace my recovery and encourage peers to do same in order to help themselves and other peers.

*****

January 17, 2013

Helping vs. Enabling

I think some of my best ideas come to me during the night or while I am in bed. I got an idea about a blog topic that I could not shake and I had to get out of bed early to write down my thoughts while. I'll start with a brief history with my English literature teacher from high school:

I always liked to write and to journal. During the last part of high school and early college, my teachers and professors complimented me on my writing. I had the same English Literature teacher my junior and senior year of high school-Mrs. Parker. I really liked her because she challenged me, and she liked me too because I was a good student academically, and was more mature compared to my peers. Sometimes I would share my problems with her and she would listen and provide feedback.

She sponsored an activity I created during black history month, a trivial game for students to participate in and to win prizes. I came up with brief summaries of famous African American people who made an impact on society and randomly followed up with questions about the individual during the month of February so that my peers could answer the questions by going to Mrs. Parker and receive a prize. This information was provided during morning announcements. So this was my relationship with Mrs. Parker.

Despite my ability to articulate thoughts and understandings of the literature I read, I remember one time my writing was not up to par and Mrs. Parker let me know it. One day, Mrs. Parker asked me to stay after class to discuss my essay. She started off by my telling me she was going to give me a "B" on my paper because she liked me, but could not because I did not show understanding of the story. She explained to me what the author's message was through the main character. By her honesty and accurate grading of my paper-giving me a "D"-she helped me understand the material and let me know I was not going to get off easy because we were "friends." She had high expectations of me which I appreciated.

Moving along to the topic of mental health related concerns, despite knowing that a loved one has a mental illness, I have heard from some family members that their relative would not take their loved one who is struggling with mental illness to the hospital because they loved them and did not want to leave them in that environment. The loved one may even know that they have a mental illness, but are not ready or willing to move forward in their recovery, with the encouragement of their family,

*****

January 17, 2013

A New Culture of Recovery

There is a stigma against me and my peers, but there is also one against mental health care providers. Common stigmas of me and my peers vary from lazy, possessing a split personality, to mass murderer-ugh! The stigma of health care providers is that they abuse patients, treat us all the same, and do not listen to patients' concerns.

However, I view my peers and health care providers totally differently. I see my peers living independently or contributing to the household. They seem like peaceful individuals-practicing mindfulness and keeping to themselves, not inflicting pain on anyone or starting a riot. They engage in creative hobbies, such as art or poetry, and other activities. My peers not only help themselves, but also other peers by offering advice and a listening ear. And they are far from lazy! A lot of the people I associate with who have a mental illness volunteer. They also work jobs that they take pride in and enjoy.

Despite what really goes on in the mental health community, a majority of our society views us differently, but why? Why don't they acknowledge us striving to live "normal" lives? How can they overlook the creativity we add to our culture...? Is it really fear? Ignorance? Or a preference in order to have a false sense of seniority? Or all that combined? Sad. It is not sad for us (people directly impacted by mental illness), but sad for them because they are losing out on great relationships, conversations, and understanding of people with different experiences from them.

A Certified Peer Specialist (CPS) training I attended last week reminded everyone in the room that providers have helped each us in some way to reach recovery. In my experience with the mental health care system, providers enjoy their jobs. They even had discussions with my mother to help her to have a better understanding of what I am going through. They do not talk to me like I am a child. Instead they provide resources to guide me to get the full benefit of recovery with outside supports. In fact, my state hospital doctor told me I could go back to college. My therapist recommended I become a CPS, a peer who acts as a liaison between staff and peers in order to help others in recovery.

Today, I did a presentation with a peer to a group of providers at an Atlanta hospital in the behavior health care unit. They were very interested in our stories and interactive. They came off as very passionate about their jobs and wanted to help patients ... So why is there this belief that they are not encouraging or supportive of our recovery?

In my experience from California and Georgia, peers are not dangerous or lazy. Don't get me wrong, I know there are peers out there who can fit the stigmatizing description like the isolated few among the general public, but the truth is most do not. And I believe my peers who have had horrible experiences with their provider, but the truth is the mental health system is changing-for the better. It is not like it was centuries ago, or even 30 years ago. Even the language within the mental health field is adopting new standards. For example, instead of calling a patient, "schizophrenic" or "bipolar" we are saying someone living with (diagnosis)... Nice. I used to use those terms, but now I avoid them because I am not my illness, I am Ashley living with an illness called schizophrenia.

Stop spreading stigmatizing messages and language— we are in a new era, a new outlook on the culture of recovery; it can only get better with us sticking together like we do online, and I am loving it!

"I like the emphasis you put on changing our language - the way we talk about our mental illnesses, and how we name ourselves. Words are so powerful, and using more positive language is something we all can do." Anonymous blogger

"One of the most amazing things to me is stigma within one's own family. I was called a lot of names and told that I had "believed a lie that the doctor's told me." I was also expected to snap back to normal quickly and get back to work. Two family members were especially harsh with me.

People seem to settle for things they make up in their heads and stuff they have heard in the media or skimmed in an article. My biggest support has been my close friends, one family member and my mental health team.

I have been schizoaffective with paranoia and PTSD for over 20 years. I have learned a lot over the years of how to listen to my body, to observe my moods and thoughts and to take care of myself physically and mentally.

I am grateful for my supporters and for people like you, who are working to knock out the stigma and educate people. Thank you!" Anonymous blogger

*****

ABOUT AUTHOR

Ashley Smith was born in Honolulu, Hawaii in 1986. She was diagnosed with schizophrenia in 2007. She works diligently to maintain recovery, and to support others affected by mental illness. Her blog, *Overcoming Schizophrenia,* was established in 2008. In 2009, she founded Embracing My Mind, Inc. a self-help organization that offers workshops and referrals.

In 2012, she became a Certified Peer Specialist (CPS) through the Georgia Mental Health Consumer Network, Inc. Currently, Ashley shares her story with the support of the Respect Institute of Georgia, and the National Alliance on Mental Illness presentation, In Our Own Voice (IOOV). Furthermore, Ashley trains peers how to share their story. Ashley was voted in to serve NAMI Georgia as a board member.

Her story was featured in the Janssen Pharmaceuticals documentary, *Living with Schizophrenia: A Call for Hope and Recovery.* She was also featured on CNN Human Factor with Sanjay Gupta. Ashley Smith is a mother and resides in Atlanta, Georgia. To contact Ashley Smith write: PO Box 115240, Atlanta, GA 30310. To get more information about Ashley visit her blog at overcomingschizophrenia.blogspot.com

*****

Made in the USA
Middletown, DE
14 July 2021